COACHING AS A
SIDE HUSTLE

SEAN WEAFER

First published by Sean Weafer, 2020

Copyright © 2020 Sean Weafer

ISBN 978-1-838-28810-5

Author: Sean Weafer

Cover Design and Typesetting by Gregg Davies Media
(www.greggdavies.com)

Additional copies of this book can be purchased
from all leading book retailers worldwide.

CONTENTS

FOREWORD

FROM THE ORIGINAL BUSINESS COACHING
REVOLUTION 2001 BOOK BY DR DENIS WAITLEY

Because you are reading this foreword, I am assuming that you bought this book, were given it as a gift, have borrowed it or are browsing through it to see if you want to add it to your library. By reading it and internalising the principles herein, you will be gaining 'The Edge' over your competitors.

There is a fine line, a winner's edge, separating the top 5 per cent in the champion's circle – the real achievers – from the rest of society. On the PGA tour, only a few strokes per year separate the top money earners from the rest of the touring professionals. In the World Cup and Olympic Games the only difference between the trophy and gold medal winners and the non-medal winners is a fraction of time, distance and points.

So it is in business and your personal life, where the playing field is anything but level. The consistent, enduring leaders in professional and personal arenas have special knowledge, attitudes, skills and habits in common that make them uncommonly successful. Their advantage is not based upon talent, IQ or luck but rather on decisions and actions that have become an integral part of their daily lives.

In a world where everyone is at risk and employment is not guaranteed, in order to get ahead today, individuals must reinvent themselves as companies and institutions restructure the way they function.

In the past, change in business and social life was incremental, and a set of personal strategies for achieving excellence was not required. Today, in the knowledge-based world where the shelf life of your formal education is no more than eighteen months and where change is the rule, a set of personal strategies is essential to success, even survival. Never again will you be able to go to your place of business on autopilot, comfortable and secure that the organisation will provide for and look after you.

In order to lead others, we must first lead ourselves. In order to gain the confidence and respect of others, we must first set a positive example. You and I must look in the mirror when we ask who is responsible for our success or failure.

In a world in which working with other people is essential, lifelong learning means deepening your understanding of yourself and others. A shared belief emerged from a recent round-table discussion among a group of innovative multi-national business leaders. All the leaders, while innovating in their business lives, were doing the same in other spheres of their lives. They agreed that their subordinates' executive growth depended on personal growth and that those who believed they had completed their education were on a fast track to personal obsolescence. Lifelong learning, once a luxury for the few, has become absolutely vital to continued success.

In my work with Apollo astronauts and Olympic athletes, I have discovered the critical role that coaches and mentors play in their achievements. The true mission of a great coach is to help uncover and develop the potential of the individual toward peak performance.

Sean Weafer has become an outstanding coach and mentor. He has the ability to assimilate complex concepts in human behaviour and convert them into interesting and informative lessons in leadership. Oceans apart in our environmental and cultural upbringing, Sean and I have experienced synergy together in an unspoken professional partnership and peer relationship in helping leaders lead.

His book is on target and laser accurate. There never was a winner who didn't have a winning coach.

As you read and grasp the underlying significance of the principles in the pages that follow, you will understand – as I have – that we are accelerating in fast forward into a world where experts, who defend what they have learned, are dinosaurs; and where coaches and those who are 'coachable' will rule the future.

Dr Denis Waitley
Author of The Psychology of Winning

C.A.S.H: COACHING AS A SIDE HUSTLE

I have been a professional coach running a successful private practice since 1997.

Well, maybe not so much the first year as I had to cold call for a year to get my first client. Even then I couldn't invoice the service as 'coaching' as executives and professionals at the time didn't know what coaching was, so we just invoiced it as 'management development'. At the time, there was also no such thing as life or personal coaching, just your therapist!

I wasn't very happy

In 1997 I was running a training company as three years before I had come out of the IT industry to partner up to create a training firm that delivered sales and management training.

Having qualified as an engineer originally I had been educated to look for 'measured outcomes' from any intervention. At that time, there was a 'sheep dip' approach to a lot of corporate training, sort of 'just send them all on the workshop and some of it will stick'. Back then, there were no readily available scoring systems or reliable forms of measurement for training. As a guy who craved specific outcomes, I was not a happy bunny with that approach.

The man who would change it for me

However in 1997 I met the man who would change that for me. That man was Dr. Denis Waitley, an American author, speaker, psychologist and performance consultant to the astronauts on the NASA Moon landings and the US Olympic Team, one hell of a gentleman and the best public speaker I have ever heard. A man uniquely ahead of his time, I had the great privilege of working with Denis over a few years from when we first met in 1997.

Now by then I had already also trained as an analytical hypnotherapist, a psychotherapist and a master practitioner of NLP (Neuro Linguistic Programming) so I had some additional tools at my disposal. However Denis nudged me in a brand new direction when he mentioned coaching.

It was like the lights came on and all the bells and whistles sounded for me. Like everything just suddenly came together and made sense. By the time I met Denis again I had brought all my engineering, psychotherapy, sales, management and entrepreneurial experience together to create a coaching system I called the G2S (or 'Global to Specific') coaching system.

Every client, every time

Years later I have tens of thousands of hours under my belt using this CPD certified system to coach C-Suite level leaders, partners in practice, mid-level managers and sales teams and training others as effective and professional coaches and mentors. There is a clear process and provenance behind it, a system by which it is applied and a means of delivering and measuring successful coaching outcomes for every client, every time.

However you are reading this book because you're interested in whether you should consider coaching as a full or part-time career or as an additional skill in a current leadership career. If so, then my response would be to absolutely look at coaching as a path (or a role skill) either as a full or successful part-time career or 'side hustle'.

You as a Coach

There are lots of reasons to train as a professional (specifically executive or business) coach.

You might be a HR professional or a business leader who wants to add executive coaching to your skillsets for the business or firm so that when all the transactional stuff gets replaced by AI (artificial intelligence), then your personal value as an executive who actively enhances, supports and guides staff and teams to greater productivity and personal development is recognised, valued and retained. Or you can choose to leave the role and do it for yourself.

You might be facing involuntary redundancy or future retirement and want to create a profitable 'side hustle' of applying your business or life expertise in a new, financially rewarding and flexible way. One that secures your future work and financial security and offers more options for life.

You might be a consultant or an accountant who wants to add it your portfolio of services or streams of income.

You might even have dreamed of and are committed to building a full-time, full-on coaching practice by which you can manifest all your ability, expertise and skills in a business that is of service to others.

Personally I love to coach. I happen to specialise in executive and business coaching (I differentiate 'executive coaching' as coaching delivered to support teams and middle-senior executives within a medium-large business setting and 'business coaching' as coaching being delivered to support business owners, entrepreneurs and partners in practice) and training and mentoring other coaches.

I love the way I can help people overcome self-limiting beliefs, a sense of overwhelm, a lack of focus or even a lack of key management, sales or communications skills, to build their personal brands, get recognised, boost their sales, prosperity and achieve more personal and job satisfaction.

I love the way that by working with me they accomplish things that would have taken them two or three times as long to get done or may never even have happened at all. I love the way they become laser focused, highly proactive, reinvigorated about their work, confident and successful. I love my career and you will too.

Coaching in the Digital Age

Since the Covid19 crisis I'm online and global now. My clients are in multiple countries, mainly Europe and North America. With G2S I have a coaching model that is highly effective for my clients. More importantly when everyone was 'working from home' or 'sheltering in place' the value of online coaching and the synergy of social media and technology helped clients overcome any residual resistance to coaching being delivered remotely.

That presents a fantastic opportunity for people considering coaching as a part or full time career and it means you don't even have to leave an existing role, at least not until you're ready to choose. You can be very successful as a professional coach in any field as a 'side hustle'.

Let's look at some of the advantages of working as a professional coach.

. . .

New Models of Working and Lifestyle

Firstly, it means there is no travel time to work with clients. You can hop on and hop off a call and you are wherever you choose to be. You can coach in the mornings, evenings, lunchtime or weekends and build a very successful practice in the process. Online coaching has tremendous flexibility for your life and that of your clients.

Secondly, the world is yours. There is nothing stopping you (with a little cultural education and sensitivity) from coaching people in the Americas, Europe, Asia, Africa, Middle East or Australia.

Thirdly, social media allows you greater global reach than ever before and communications platforms such as Zoom, Teams and others allow you to be highly mobile and run a successful coaching business (or coach a distributed remote-working team) from anywhere in the world (with internet access) so you can live the life of a 'digital nomad' if you choose.

Think about that. As an online G2S coach your business can be anywhere, your home can be anywhere and it can be a lucrative full or part-time career.

Becoming a G2S Coach

So who should consider being a coach then? The people that I personally train and mentor in my system are a mix of:

1. Professionals or consultants who want to add an additional revenue stream to their business.
2. Executives looking at getting out or retiring from the corporate world and want a part or full-time flexible business model that drives significant revenue and more control.
3. Professionals who want to change to working from home

and the flexibility to spend more time with their families or older relatives.

4. Leaders who want to apply a more entrepreneurial and innovative approach to leading their teams and organisations.
5. Experts who want to develop their expertise into a thriving service business.
6. Previously certified coaches who want to up their skills and revenues.

Speaking from Experience

There are some things you do need to think about.

Firstly, one needs to get a good education as a coach in a robust and proven coaching system.

Secondly, one needs to be clear as to what kind of coach you want to be. Choose a niche. The sooner you pick a space the quicker you can be up serving it and creating an income. Ideally pick a niche that aligns with your experience, expertise and enthusiasm.

Third, consider joining a professional coaching body. Do you absolutely need to be a member of a professional body such as the International Coach Federation, European Mentoring and Coaching Council etc? Probably not. However as the industry continues to professionalize then it's probably worth considering.

Personally, I was a Founder Member and Honorary VP of the Association for Coaching in the UK when it started but for many years after I left I wasn't a member of any such body. Your call. Some companies when they tender for their coaching panels I've been told do ask for it but none that I've ever met at the time of writing.

. . .

A "Lucrative Part-Time Career"

My wife has always called my coaching business a "lucrative part-time career" as I always seem to have a lot more time to do stuff than she does in her work (hence the book's title: 'C.A.S.H: Coaching As a Side-Hustle'!).

Professional G2S coaching is, at its best, a structured system and a clear set of skills to turn your unique business or leadership expertise into a way of helping a particular set of people to actualise their full potential and be paid for it.

My work is in training coaches in a specific system that delivers guaranteed results every time to their clients. Does it matter what their area of expertise is? Not really. It can be executive and business, sales, technology, life coaching, personal coaching, spiritual, wellbeing and health or any area in which you have expertise that might benefit from a system to convert it into a business.

I happen to specialise in coaching and mentoring in business (executive, leadership, sales, management, communications etc.). Why? Because it's my primary area of expertise. Do I do personal coaching? Yes. Do I do spiritual coaching? Yes. (See my book 'Invoking the Feminine: Strength, Love and Wisdom') but business is my primary niche.

Businesses (particularly medium-large companies) value coaching and mentoring as critical skills for their leaders and managers. In addition, they understand the value of coaching for their executives and their teams, they have a budget for it, they have vetted coaching panels you can apply for and they usually provide a lot of referred business from within the firm if they are of any size.

That means that you can charge a good professional fee (certainly one that will get you over the magical 'six figure fee' if you're prepared to work hard at it). However you also need to appreciate

7

that if you want to be a busy and successful coach then you have *got* to be able to sell.

Just getting trained (or certified) as a coach does not guarantee your success. You need to be able to sell your services too.

The busiest coaches, those earning the real money, are the ones who are able to actively sell their services. That can be hard as you really are 'selling yourself' and for many of us that's something new and it takes a while to come to terms with. However the good news is that selling and marketing your coaching services can be taught along with pricing, presentations and all the tips and techniques that can turn you into a highly trusted asset to a company or private client.

In the G2S coach training program we don't just train our coaches, we also take them through a communications program that helps them with building their own coaching practice but also equips them to share these valuable skills with their own clients.

So, What's the Catch?

Are there down-sides to coaching as a career? Definitely. There are so many people out there as coaches of various forms that it is a very crowded market place and it can be hard to differentiate yourself from the white noise around you.

It can be lonely just working on your own so being a member of some form of a network or master mind group can be a big help. The community you want to find however is the one that resonates most with you.

Keeping yourself motivated, organised, getting your admin done, getting your website built, keeping your social media presence up and running, selling, getting your first contacts with decision-makers. Going into your next session of the day when you're tired or when your emotional state is not as strong as it should be. There's a lack of financial security or sometimes monthly cash flow can be stressful. There are challenges.

However, it can be a lot less challenging if you start by looking at coaching as a second career, a home or travel-based digital business, a retirement profession or a lucrative side-hustle and then the rewards can outweigh the challenge and it becomes your 'portable or portfolio profession'. However many of us do run successful full-time practices too. It depends entirely on you and your vision for your future.

If that vision includes more freedom, personal control, mobility, income (there are all sorts of business and income models), a high degree of personal satisfaction when you've been of service to others or helped to make a powerful change or life shift for someone and a greater sense of personal fulfilment, then coaching is for you.

If after reading all this coaching (full or part-time, as a solopreneur or as a leader or corporate manager or as an executive or life coach) as a career or skill is still something you're interested in, then read on and let's start preparing you for your new career or additional 'stream-of-income' side hustle as a professional coach.

2

WHY COACHING?

"We are beings caught between peaks of unlimited consciousness and deep valleys of self-limiting imaginings."

In this chapter I want to look at some of the reasons why coaching is such a powerful intervention for enabling change and growth in a person's life but also for driving performance and success in business.

Imagine a world where people are happy in their roles, effective in their work, self-directed in their efforts and living more fulfilled personal lives or relationships. Imagine people effortlessly managing stressful environments, making effective decisions, taking actions without hesitation, communicating clearly, living more balanced lives and maximizing their personal and spiritual potential for achievement on a consistent basis.

In business, imagine a world that uses the benefits of AI and digital technology and marries it seamlessly to the people and emotional skills of powerful influence, creating collaborative, inclusive, co-creative and highly productive workplaces. Imagine if all business leaders were not just technically expert but highly influential, empathic and co-creative, able to effortlessly empower their teams to contribute not just some but all of their potential.

Business coaching (in all its forms leadership, management, executive, sales, presentation etc.) is about effective and efficient individual, team and organisational performance. It's a shift in business management culture effected at an individual level that profoundly impacts on the organization as a whole. It does this through achieving consistent, specific and measurable results from people in a consultative, non-directive way; a way that gathers the very best of the coach and the individual being coached and forges it into something greater than either would have accomplished alone.

It is how management can come to delegate more effectively, through switching on the desire of their staff to initiate change willingly. It enables individual business leaders to realise their potential to achieve higher levels of personal and business performance. It raises levels of individual commitment to personal and corporate success and it helps unleash the true potential of the person being coached.

Coaching leaders (and leaders coaching their teams) is about harmonising the goals of the individual and the organisation. Coaching is increasingly accepted as a skill all managers and leaders should have and should practise with staff particularly where teams are working remotely but often coaching has been viewed as a 'competency' of management rather than as a style of management itself.

Coaching is leadership for the new digital age. An age where leadership has moved from a simple 'command and control' directive and expertise-based model to an 'advisor model' of engagement, partnership and service to the team through influence and facilitation. A world in which the purpose of the leader is to create the environment in which their people can excel.

Now imagine a world in which in our personal lives and workplace we can get access to quality coaching professionals with expertise in personal wellbeing, or nutrition or fitness, or life and personal skills, finance, career skills, goal-setting, healing, spiritual or counselling skills who use an effective process of helping their clients design their futures and then create them through accountable actions.

Picture the difference in our confidence, our relationships, our career and prosperity, in fact all aspects of our lives enhanced and actualised by working with a well-trained life or personal coach. Imagine the power and personal satisfaction and fulfilment that can be unleashed in our lives and careers by working with such a coach.

Good coaching engages people in a systematic process and a discipline focused on personal excellence and success. The ultimate goal of this process is the personal fulfilment and empowerment of the individual being coached and the consistent achievement of their goals as the result of this. In many ways coaching is a process that helps us take our imagination and manifest it in the real world through a systematic process of reflection, clarity and action.

Good coaching also takes into consideration a critical element of personal and business success, the *personal meaning* attached to the actions that create this success by the person undertaking the action.

We have all at one time paused to admire the challenges that successful people faced and overcame in their pursuit of business excellence and sporting or personal success. The general assumption tends to be that they have been exceptional in some way, or just lucky, by being in the right place at the right time. Yet luck is often defined as "when preparation meets opportunity". The defining characteristic of a person's "overnight success" often seems to be that it takes years of personal preparation and experience on the part of that person to recognise and grasp the opportunity when it presents itself. If so, then something else is at work that allows such successful people to forge their way to the top in business and life.

I suggest that the critical factor that empowers the results that successful coaches get from their clients is personal meaning, the prime and emotional value that we attach to the decisions that we make and to the actions that we take. The 'Why?'.

As a result, the theoretical models that I use to design my G2S coach training and coaching services are threefold. The first model is based on the inherent desire for a client to self-actualise or to be the best they can be and to see meaning in that purpose.

This is based on the work of Abraham Maslow, whose theory of the Hierarchy of Needs proposes that the desire for humans to self-actualise is the highest of all needs. This, I believe is the essence of mankind's search for meaning and it is what drives us to higher and higher levels of evolution. It could be considered as a driver towards excellence that is 'hard-wired' into our psychological and behavioural systems. I personally believe that this desire to self-actualise, to fulfil our purpose, to be all that we can be is driven by a greater 'spiritual' purpose and the need to evolve.

The second model concerns the ability to change the client's perspective on, or perception of, the context or environment in which they may find themselves when they first come to coaching. By being able to change a client's perception of their context or situation a coach can help them to generate new solutions to old challenges, much like one's levels of stress changes as one changes one's attitude to the stressor. This model draws from the work of Carl Jung, whose work in the fields of human preferences and perception is used in many areas.

The third model is that of excellence in communication and influence both with oneself and with others: with oneself, to gain a greater sense of self awareness and motivation; and with others, to gain the ability to communicate clearly one's needs and to harmonise them with the needs of others for maximum performance and influence.

This third model is based on the skills of Neuro Linguistic Programming (NLP), a field that focuses on, among other things, the development of effective communications processes and performance. The area of NLP is recognized as a rich field of techniques and models that assist us to evolve our thinking to higher levels, to gain a greater sense of self-understanding, to gain greater control over our personal states (or emotions, which drive our decisions and hence our actions) and provide the tools necessary to communicate the realisations of that self-understanding to the people around us.

At this point, we might pause to consider what NLP stands for:

N stands for Neuro or the neural system (including the brain, spinal cord and radial nerves) the many live nerve connections of which our human system is composed. So dense is this number of live nerve connections that it was once 'guestimated' by neurobiologists at somewhere in the region of 10 to the power of 10. This number is supposedly greater than the number of every grain of sand on every beach and desert in the world today and all of this in the body of just one human being. To quote Shakespeare's Hamlet "What a piece of work is Man".

L stands for Linguistics, which has to do with language, how we use it, the pictures it paints in our minds and how our behaviours are affected by these holistic pictures that create behavioural responses. Imaging for a moment you sitting in your favourite restaurant, choosing your favourite dish from the menu and remembering how it tastes and now notice your response: you 'see' and 'smell' the food, and your mouth begins to water yet it's only words on a page, not the food itself, that is in front of us. The words have caused the physiological response.

P stands for Programming. This relates to the 'strategies' that people use in everything they do, from making decisions about how they eat their food to decisions about life and business. When you eat a meal do you leave your favourite item on the plate until last or do you take a little bit of it to complement the food on the plate that you like least? Do you know anyone who will not eat their morning toast unless it's buttered right out to the edges?

Everyone uses strategies that are unique to them. Through coaching we sometimes need to challenge and reframe those strategies if they are not supportive of the desired performance of the client.

Coaching has evolved into many forms by recognizing collaboration rather than simple direction as a basis for individual excellence. Perhaps the most usual form of coaching that we are familiar with is the relationship between a sports coach and the athlete. This relationship is based on a mutual trust and exchange of information for the benefit of the athlete's performance. With the help of a sports coach, the athlete learns to maximise their physical and mental potential to a higher degree than that which they might otherwise have reached on their own.

We have only to look at the top athletes in the arena of sports today from golf to basketball to see the effect an inspiring, challenging and knowledgeable coach can have on the performance of an athlete.

Present-day sports coaches are a different breed. While much emphasis in sports coaching is still placed on the physical and technical aspect of the game now equal emphasis is placed on a more vital factor, the mental strategies that create the winning edge that sets the superstars of sport apart from the mainstream.

In fact, it is not unusual to find coaches who specialize in just the 'mind game' rather than the physical game. A critical element of that mental edge is the emotional energy that the athlete empowers their actions with, energy drawn from the meaning or value they place on their success.

Coaching is based on this same principle, that of honing the mindset of a client so that they can marshal their mental and physical resources to achieve more than they would working alone.

In business it plays an increasingly important part in delivering measurable and tangible results to teams and colleagues who face greater and greater challenges in maximising their potential, within ever more limiting time frames. In our personal lives faced with even more change, disruption, stresses and challenges coaching can empower and support us to forge lives that are not just successful but significant.

To meet challenges, smart people turn to a professional coach whose job is to ensure a clear answer to the following question:

'What one thing could you do, such that if you were to do it, it would affect the greatest amount of change for you right now?'

It is worth reading that again. In that one question is the essence of the challenge that faces us all: focusing on the most important thing we should be doing all the time; being all that we can be.

This begins the process of helping the client to start to control their focus and intent and brings two additional key factors, that of accountability and an external view for effective feedback and corrective action. All these things come from effective coaching.

However, it often seems that a clear definition of coaching today is lacking. Therefore, let me offer a specific definition of coaching and then clarify how it differs from both mentoring and therapy of any kind. In my personal view coaching may be defined thus:

Coaching is a collaborative partnership between a coach and a client and a system that identifies perceived obstacles, generates solutions, sets objectives and implements actions based on personal accountability.

It is worth exploring this definition further. By **collaborative** I mean that coaching is something that relies on the synergy of two people to accomplish more than either would alone. Two minds working on one agenda, creating a 'third mind' from which often comes insights and inspirations that otherwise may never be had by an individual working alone.

It is a **system** because it utilises a structure and sequence that leads to the definition and solution of **perceived** obstacles.

By **perceived** I mean that often a person may be finding some difficulty in handling certain challenges because they are caught up in the immediate perspective and the potential consequences of the challenge. By being able to change their perspective or their way of looking at the challenge, a coach can often assist their client to find new solutions or new ways of overcoming such challenges. I sometimes call this the "crossword syndrome".

Have you ever attempted a crossword and found yourself stuck on one word, just one word that would open up the solution to the crossword? No matter how hard you try you cannot find that word and then someone leans over your shoulder, reads the clue and gives you the answer and suddenly, seemingly without effort, they have resolved the problem? That's because that person was able to take a 'meta view' of the problem.

This 'meta' view is one that is above the immediate perspective of the problem as it does not emotionally impact on that person's success or failure. As such the other person was able to find the solution that helped, as there is no loss to them or implied threat if they were to get their answer or suggestion wrong.

Coaches, not personally impacted by the consequences of the client's challenge, often provide such 'meta views' to their clients.

Solution, Objective and Action, the process by which a coach breaks the global challenge into the 'bite size' pieces from which all great endeavours can be accomplished. Michael Gerber, author of 'The E-Myth' said that extraordinary businesses are not accomplished by extraordinary people; they are accomplished by ordinary people who do ordinary things extraordinarily well. Simple actions and simple processes mean guaranteed results.

Lastly, **Accountability** is the key to coaching success. The willingness of the client to be held *accountable to themselves by the coach* for delivering on their actions in which they play a part in defining. Without the disciplined and external input of the coach and the willingness of the client to allow the coach *to hold them personally accountable* for the actions taken (or not) then the coaching process would fail.

So, how does coaching differ from mentoring and therapy? First, coaching differs from business mentoring in that coaching is *non-role or industry specific*. In other words it is focused on the person and not the job role or skills that the person that is being coached (the 'client', as opposed to the 'sponsor' or organisation they work for) is doing.

Coaches focus on the overall development and empowerment of the individual and not necessarily job specific skills. As part of the process, they consider the additional resources or training that a person may need to be successful, although the coach does not necessarily provide such training (although they may).

The coach focuses on the development of the *person* not the *role*. As such, someone trained in coaching can be brought in to make change anywhere. They effect change in the role by developing *the individual* and their performance, not necessarily the role itself.

In most cases, an executive or business coach may have little or no knowledge of the specifics of the role carried out by the client unless it is relevant to the client's objectives. It is the client who brings change to their role. It is the empowerment of the client that returns power to the individual to actively engage in effecting positive and productive change, something that is as true in personal/life coaching as it is in business. This is typically why professional coaches are brought into companies to work at middle-senior executive levels where the client already has significant job or role experience but the challenge might lie in communications, interpersonal skills, performance, mindset, motivation, time or boundary management etc.

In business mentoring, while the same techniques of engagement can be used, the emphasis is different. Here the emphasis is very much **on the passing on of a specific skill-set or culturally specific knowledge for a particular role**. Here the mentor may provide highly specific skills education and will primarily focus on the development of the *skills and experience* needed for the role and not necessarily the person. In most cases a mentor is someone who is senior to the team member or mentee and has previously been successful in the role.

The difference between life or personal coaching and therapy is more distinct. In a very simplified definition (with apologies to professional therapists) it would be that **therapy is a process focused on resolving issues that occurred in the past (or 'root causes') that effect current behaviours**. The emphasis is on identifying and resolving the emotional or psychological issues that, once resolved, can improve the present behaviour or wellbeing of the person. Therapy, of necessity, looks into the past and the conditioning that created the present behaviour with a view to resolving those issues.

Coaching however is a process that focuses on the client's **present situation** to deliver better **future outcomes.** It focuses on the future and the present decisions that create it.

So who is using coaching today? Everyone from business owners, chief executives and senior directors to middle managers, team leaders and sales people in business benefit from using professional external coaches today. For life or personal coaches, people who want to make career or relationship changes, or want to fulfil more of their energy, fitness, relationship, finance, or potential and personal growth. For each one the need for the coach is different.

From a business perspective (as this is my specific area of expertise) often for business owners, C Suite leaders and Heads of Function, coaching serves as a partnership to help them focus their thinking on the organisation and acts as a sounding board for their ideas, even generating new ideas and helping them focus on more effective planning and communication strategies for their organisations. It helps overcome a lot of the isolation felt by such executives and holds them accountable for continued innovation within the company. It can often start out with very specific objectives but evolve into a more conversational, observational and support-based engagement.

For senior directors and managers, apart from the challenge of working "on" rather than "in" their teams or departments, managing their boundaries and getting more team performance there are often issues dealing with their positioning, recognition and personal branding within the firm that they need to address.

Team leaders, often plucked from the floor and given responsibility without a lot of prior preparation may need support in communications or in the development of a coaching culture within their teams that assists in the learning of positive processes by which they can lead and empower in a consultative manner, people who may have until recently been their peers.

For sales people the emphasis is often on personal focus, clarity, confidence and enhanced communications and influencing skills, raising the standards for them, leading them to results beyond those they would have achieved alone, encouraging them to develop and apply their personal abilities to accomplish measurable and quantifiable increases in their sales and profitability.

In all cases, coaching brings the synergy and the accountability to effect change. What effects change at a personal level, the leverage, is uniquely different in each case and I train coaches to identify, access and use that leverage to effect the desired change.

In effect, coaches act as catalysts of change first by helping a client to identify their desired outcomes and then by providing a specific process to effect the action that brings change. After the action is initiated they engage in a process of accountability and of reinforcing and balancing feedback to keep their client on track to reach the goals that have been mutually defined.

The demand for properly trained professional coaches is increasing all the time as the market for coaching globally continues to expand. The consultancy firm PwC has indicted that the coaching industry is the second fastest growing industry in the world and now that the world has fully embraced digital working, our clients are global.

The simple fact that people can have access to an external or objective overview, free of the limiting thoughts and views that, of necessity, often define a person's role or personal life and free of any other agenda other than their success, is very powerful and helps create rapid and lasting change.

For coaches, the fact that they bring a positive expectation of the results of coaching for their clients (either personal or professional) and a system by which it can be achieved, sets their client up for personal or professional success every time.

3

A BRIEF HISTORY OF BUSINESS COACHING

With apologies to my readers who may see themselves as primarily life or personal coaches, in this chapter I wanted to briefly explore the evolution of business coaching as we understand it today. In truth, life and personal coaching has matched the growth of business coaching since its inception in the late 90's. In fact, it is probably fair to say that life coaching was starting to evolve even before business coaching became recognized as the 'game changing' intervention it is today.

Also, many of the conditions within the modern workplace continue to create the opportunities for personal or life coaching as people seek out career coaching, confidence coaching or stress management and personal wellbeing.

Business (Leadership or Executive) coaching as it is also known, became one answer to the increasing problem of less time and more demands within all forms of business venture, whether they are team driven corporations or owner-managed smaller enterprises.

But there are other problems manifesting themselves within the work environment that coaching can address: problems such as the greater utilization of human capital and the coming to terms with changed social dynamics and values of the workplace that conditions the behaviour of such capital.

These changes in social dynamics have resulted in less respect for and trust in authority for authority's sake, less willingness to accept directive rather than co-operative management structures, less staff loyalty to the company leading to greater mobility in the workforce and a greater appreciation by the staff of their individual identity. This increasingly is manifesting itself in a desire for more flexible working hours (hence increasingly remote or teleworking, four-day weeks and paternity leave are now a part of corporate life) greater recognition for personal contribution and respect of personal values.

Why are these issues presenting themselves at this time? To find the answer we need to look briefly at the bigger social picture and the effects of better education, the media's creation of higher expectations and the increasing search for greater meaning and value in people's lives.

In the mid-20th century the numbers moving from primary to secondary and then on to tertiary education were comparatively few compared to the numbers that enjoy such opportunities now. The foundation of widespread and generally free education in the West has provided higher standards of education to a larger group of people than ever before in the history of society. It has provided the education that has fuelled the digital age and the move from an industrial-based society to a society where one of the most important forms of business capital is that of information and knowledge and increasingly, the ability to project personal and professional influence.

Education is an important factor in the conditioning that creates our values and hence our beliefs. Our conditioning comes from many sources: apart from education, our social situation, family structure, spiritual beliefs, peers and so on are all contributing factors. All of the above have undergone significant change in the last few decades. In addition, the 'pillars of society' (church, state, media, big business and so on) in which people traditionally placed in a great deal of trust have been found lacking too often for that faith and trust to remain as it was in previous generations.

This loss of faith in centuries-old models of behaviour has caused an increase in the number of people seeking their own answers, finding their own path to meaning in their life and work. It has also resulted in a more challenging attitude towards authority. In the past, people would seldom question the word of a teacher, policeman, politician or a professional such as a lawyer, barrister, accountant or even their own 'place' in society. Now that has changed. The impact of this social change is being felt in the workplace where the role of the leader is also, of necessity, in a process of change along with the multi-generational make-up of the workplace and the new digital and remote workspace.

Now the emphasis in leadership and management training is increasingly on people development, communications skills and relationship management. Skills that are termed the 'soft skills' of management and business were often overlooked in the traditional style of management that tended towards an authoritative and paternalistic approach.

Improved education and changed conditions have also raised our expectations above mere survival. Over the last several generations, despite war and economic recession or perhaps because of it, each generation has improved substantially above the one prior to it. The lives of our grandparents were significantly different from ours today.

Ours has become a materially richer (if more divided) society but one where consumerism and acquisition have arguably replaced the more human and community-based values of earlier generations. The media has served to fuel such material expectations and the bombardment of our homes each evening through television, radio, news print and social media has continued the rise in personal expectations.

But the rise in our expectations has also changed the nature of the relationships that we have within our workplace and indeed in our personal relationships.

In the distant past, the position of a company leader or manager was almost sacred. Management was of a style that directed an employee to perform and expected such performance without question. A manager's word was law and they decided the fate of those who worked below them. Organisations were created on an almost institutional basis. They were large, almost military-like structures whose hierarchical framework ensured that power travelled from the top down. Such organisations matched the type of society people lived in.

Only gradually, with the growth in the power of trade unionism were the individual's needs considered. But management continued to direct. Morale was never an issue: the phrase "firings will continue until morale improves" aptly sums up the attitude of the time. Loyalty to a firm was unconditionally expected. Many employees were employed from cradle to grave, held there not just by the politics of the workplace but by the expectations of a society that valued permanency and security of tenure.

At one time, the greatest hold that authoritative management had over people was the fear of losing one's job. The consequences of this, including the shame, personal devaluation and loss of social status among one's peers often associated with unemployment, were powerful motivators for compliance without question.

But by the late 20th and early 21st century economic crises, recessions, pandemics and the willingness of firms to shed people *en masse*, regardless of loyalty or years of service, resulted in a difficult awakening to the new environment of downsizing, 'zero hours' contract work, the 'gig economy' and redundancy. This awakening created a new kind of culture in the workplace, a culture in which the individual began to accept that loyalty counted for little and that they needed to look to themselves to survive the changing times ahead.

A new philosophy was starting to emerge from the past where the employee was dependant on the company for their future and security, to the present, where the employee recognises their intellectual capital is that which gives the company its strength.

Company management was learning to recognize that the success of the company was dependant on the degree of interdependence of the many skilled individuals who work together. The age of flat-lined, matrix-managed and self-directed teams was born. But these teams were no longer composed of the traditional employee profile. Something else happened in the time of recession and another new culture was born, a culture of personal enterprise and acceptance of change as a condition of the modern workplace.

The day of the contractor, the self-employed consultant, the remote-worker and the mobile employee had arrived. Increasing numbers of a new kind of employee began to enter the workplace from the downsized organisations of the past. Contractors, consultants, work outplacement specialists, who worked by the hour and who owed loyalty only to their pay cheque and themselves, began to take their place in the modern organisation, working alongside those who still held the old traditional sense of employee.

A new ethos began to enter the workplace, that of personal empowerment. The employee (now a contractor) began to see themselves as valuable in their own right as their own boss, independent of the workplace. The employee was becoming an entrepreneur and a contractor.

The concept of self-directed and flat-line managed teams was designed to bring a greater cost- effectiveness and faster management communications to companies; a better means of effecting change at a more immediate level to respond to the rapid changes in the new marketplace. In a sense it was also designed to empower the employee, as they were to be recognised as an integral part of the team. 'Team building' became the new phrase. But in the rush to embrace team building, company leaders had neglected a number of important components in making their teams work.

The first was the effect that the new form of team structure, which did away with the many layers of hierarchical privilege that had previously existed, would have on existing leaders and managers.

This new structure placed senior management for the first time in face-to-face, frontline, operational roles. The effect was enormous on veteran managers used to direction and obedience, suddenly working closer than ever with employees whose expectations had changed, who now viewed themselves as inherently valuable, whose sense of loyalty was no longer to the company but to themselves and who were becoming increasingly more mobile in the marketplace.

Traditional leadership training was inadequate to handle the changes in the work place and their proximity to people with whom they may never have had to converse in the past. Their skills were outdated and they still saw directive management continuing unchanged, unquestioned and unchecked at more senior levels.

The second was the continued growth of technology businesses. In the early days, this growth led to more technicians or even less experienced people being given management responsibility, which in the old economy would not have come their way for some time. With nothing to fall back on, a poor understanding of management and now expected to manage others who may have been their peers only yesterday, the new executives needed to find a new management system.

The third had been the dream of management for some time. This dream was that someday a way would be found to create self-empowered, self-motivated and self-directed teams that would ease the burden of managers who had come to be working more 'IN' their teams doing the work they were hiring others for, rather than 'ON' their teams, leading by example and well thought out strategies.

The fourth was the lack of a process and a discipline that would guarantee results, while allowing everyone, both management and team members, full participation and the opportunity to benefit personally, to be fulfilled in their work and, therefore, motivated by the challenges they faced as a team and as an organization.

The time had come for a new and radical approach to management. The answer was employee-centred management facilitation through a new style of manager, the manager as coach.

Senior management would still set the objectives. These objectives would then be communicated

through the organisation by coaching team members to an appreciation of the importance of their personal contribution and the personal benefit to be gained in the process of achieving corporate plans.

The age of the inhouse corporate coach had arrived, supported by external certified and experienced professional coaches who would engage and manifest the greater potential of the business's leaders and leadership team. The Age of the Coach had arrived.

4

CORE BELIEFS OF COACHING

There are a number of core concepts or beliefs about coaching that a professional coach does well to work by. The following are the most important beliefs that coaches might want to keep in mind when interfacing with their clients, team members and colleagues.

---

1. Expectations: the coach should always expect more from the client than the client believes they are capable of accomplishing themselves.

In coaching we are working towards a tangible change in both the performance and the personal perception of the client. To achieve this, it is necessary that the *coach fully expects that the client is capable of accomplishing everything they set out to achieve*. It is imperative that a coach believes that the client has all the resources they need to reach their goals or can gain these resources on the coaching journey that they are about to undertake.

We need to believe this because our expectations of the person we are working with are subtly transmitted through our voice tonality, our body language and the words we use. These things are unconsciously noticed and acted upon by our clients. *How a client perceives our expectations of them will directly impact on their self-belief and their willingness to attempt what they have never achieved on their own in the past.* Our expectations often drive a client's behaviours for if we have successfully developed excellent rapport with them, they will often want to meet those expectations as much to please us as for themselves.

Our belief in others has an impact on ourselves too, on what is termed our 'congruence'.

Congruence is that personal state when what we believe, feel and say all combine to create a powerfully credible state of communication that will always convince others of our sincerity in the process and our belief that they can successfully overcome past obstacles and power towards future success. *Our expectations of the client, therefore, become the benchmark by which the client begins to change their assessment of themselves and raise their levels of self-expectation.*

This is the only way we can begin the process of increasing the Beta (or base-line) level of performance and start to shift perceptions that may have kept a person trapped in a limited performance cycle in the past.

Changing one's expectations is a critical factor in success. If success can be defined as "the achievement of predefined goals", then the impetus for being willing to create such goals comes from believing that by raising our personal expectations of ourselves, we can accomplish something more satisfying and valuable than what we possess at present. In short, if we allow our clients or staff to set standards that they have always set in the past, they will always get what they have got in the past.

Many clients may be coming to the coaching process with personal or professional histories that have prevented them from having a strong sense of self, personal self-esteem or confidence in themselves.

Coaching exists to continuously create new standards of achievement and, therefore a coach's expectations of clients' performance should always be more than what clients have accomplished prior to working with a coach. The willingness and the ability of the client to reach new standards begins with the conviction of the coach that they can make goals into dreams with a deadline.

It is *our expectations* of our clients that drives their behaviours, their self-belief, confidence and success.

---

2. Engagement and Contracting: clients should always feel engaged in the process.

'Contracting' is a state of agreement between people, a willingness of one or the other to agree and work with the suggestions of others because they perceive a benefit from this. One could say it is the perfect state for an assertive person, who reaches their goals through influence and consultation rather than through direction and enforcement.

Effective coaches learn to 'contract' with clients very quickly in the coaching relationship. Coaches are not there to give advice but to "ask questions and make suggestions". We are there to lead others to an understanding of their own personal power, not to prove how wonderful we are as advisors.

The old adage "give a man a fish and you feed him for a day, teach him how to fish and you feed him for life" is especially true in the case of coaching. We need to quickly establish a relationship where our clients willingly work with our suggestions. It is only when we have created this that we can effect real and lasting change for them. This is accomplished first by creating strong rapport between the coach and the client, which is in turn strengthened by the confidential aspect of coaching. This builds an atmosphere of trust and mutual respect between coach and the client; an atmosphere where the client becomes more open to suggestions than they might have been prior to having a coach.

Contracting is also created by the clear understanding of the following: that the coach exists purely for the support of the client, to assist *them* to reach *their* agenda; that we as a coach (or manager engaged in coaching) only reach *our* agenda by ensuring the client or team member reaches theirs; that coaches are intimately tied to the success of their clients; and that it is truly a relationship of '*two minds working on one agenda*'.

So the clear definition of the client's agenda, their needs, desires and wants, and the successful elicitation of the values or benefits that motivate clients to drive towards these goals are critical elements in creating a powerful contract for change.

---

3. Global to Specific (G2S): breaking the inaction trance.

Many people find themselves unable or unwilling to take action to change their circumstance because they view the challenge or problem in a global sense. They focus on the enormity of the challenge (and the global consequences of failure) rather than on the first thing they need to do to effect the change that would lead to the accomplishment of this same challenge.

In coaching, our work is to help clients perceive such challenges and problems as surmountable through the completion of a succession of smaller activities. Once identified and sequenced properly, these activities are just smaller steps towards making the change they desire and achieving the greater goal.

Michael Gerber in his book, *The E-Myth*, mentions that extraordinary businesses are seldom created by extraordinary people. Rather, they are created by ordinary people who do the ordinary things extraordinarily well, mainly because good systems have been put in place that allow them to do this.

Coaching is a system of excellence that helps us all achieve extraordinary things; a system that allows us all to soar towards our personal Alpha (Flow or Fully Actualised) levels.

---

4. Transparency: no hidden agendas.

An important aspect of coaching (especially within a corporate context) is the existence of transparency in the process. By transparency I mean that both coach and client are working towards the same goal i.e. the agenda of the personal client or the executive when allied to the overall objectives of the company.

Coaching is a partnership and partners share things. The openness of the process assists rapport, trust and the free exchange of views and ideas that lead to a synergistic approach where all parties contribute.

A simple example of this is the documentation involved in coaching. The coach might for example (but not necessarily) receive a (digital or hard) copy of the work the client completes. Or any notes that the coach makes are freely shared with the client. Therefore, there is no information that both parties are not aware of. This is important because, in all circumstances, transparency is paramount within coaching.

---

5. Meaning: revealing the inner motivation.

In coaching, identifying meaning is critical. This is the power that effects the greatest change in the client. As soon as the client finds a reason, a sense of purpose, then their own internal energies will drive the process and the coach simply acts as a guide and support, while the client moves inexorably towards the fulfilment of their needs. Once the coach has identified the real meaning and benefit in the process, their hard work is often over.

Working to one's values or personal meaning is essential for success: if there is a conflict in one's values then there is no progress. A huge number of people are striving for more meaning in their life and work but are unprepared to take the responsibility that comes with that, at least not on their own.

Having a coach provides the support necessary to take on this responsibility and effect change in one's life, career and business. For those of us who wish to have more control over our relationships, careers, lives, prosperity and health or businesses, we must be willing to accept greater responsibility for the outcome of our actions. This is significantly easier and more focused when we have the help of a dedicated coach whose only agenda is that of the client's.

6. Balance: managing the consequences of progress.

Even the most positive change requires a price, which we must all be willing to pay if we want to move from one place in our life to another. For those who wish to reach more of their potential through coaching and reap the rewards that this brings with it, there can be substantial change often in a very short period of time relative to what has happened before.

However how our family, friends and colleagues view us may change as a result of our changing and we need to be prepared for that. Good coaches will encourage their clients to study the ecology of the consequences of their actions: what will they gain or lose by changing or accomplishing something? What will be required of them? What are they willing to do? And *then* what are they willing to do? Who are they really doing it for and why?

I often tell my clients that they stand on two legs: their professional leg and their personal leg. If either leg is weakened, then the ability they have to move forward is greatly reduced. Therefore, it is important to look at all potential consequences and resolve them as best as is possible, so that our client can move forward confidently to new horizons.

7. 100 per cent: the least we can give.

If we are assisting people to be the very best that they can be, then as coaches we are bound to give everything that we have to help make change. This is the 100 per cent contract that we should all enter into when coaching.

Giving 100 per cent is also in the coach's interest. After all, the client's success is directly related to our success: when they accomplish their objectives we will have played an integral part in that accomplishment.

Just like a coach who works with an athlete, life and business coaches are not the ones who win the gold medals. However, there can be a great sense of satisfaction when one reads or hears of a client or a colleague who has soared to new levels in their career as a result of our help. Most clients remember it too and it enhances our reputation, our earning power and our network of influence, ensuring our continued personal success from the success of others.

---

100 per cent – nothing less.

5

MODELS OF COACHING

Over nearly twenty five years as a professional coach I have evolved some distinct models by which we can define what is occurring within coaching and coaching's place in the modern learning organisation. These are 6C Model and the Alpha-Beta Model.

The 6C Model of Coaching:

The first model is one I've called it 'The 6C Model' and it is something that I explain to my coaching clients when explaining how coaching can deliver a real and tangible benefit to their careers or businesses.

The 6C's of the Model are: CONTEXT, CLARITY, CONTROL, CONFIDENCE, COMMUNICATION AND COMPETENCE.

1. CONTEXT: The first part of the model deals with *Context* or to be more specific, the *environment* in which we find ourselves working.

Our environment constantly changes and the pace of change may be such that we find ourselves usually *reacting* to the changes rather than being *proactive*.

We find ourselves working in a constant 'fire-fighting' mode just holding the line against the growing tide of work and the demands that our life, career or business seems to be heaping upon us. The demands placed upon us are such that little time is available for active reflection and we are driven by external forces rather than by our own inner compass or agenda.

We therefore tend to 'Reflex' or simply unconsciously respond to stimuli, when we should 'Reflect' or consciously choose the course of action that is most beneficial.

Therefore to successfully move from a Reactive state to a Proactive state we need to develop our Clarity or Focus.

2. CLARITY: No matter how busy we are we can always benefit by taking some time out for *'enforced reflection'*, a time in our diary for space and time away from our normal environment and work pressures that allows us to get a greater sense of focus and purpose. But (and be honest) when did we do that last?

Lack of clarity deprives us of the ability to focus and therefore act effectively. It maximises stress. Focus is an essential part of performance and our focus is composed of two areas, purpose and passion.

Purpose is the 'WHAT' or what we have or want to do but passion is the 'WHY' or what we personally get when we make the goal happen. When this is done correctly it ensures that any business coaching goal is directly related to the personal motivation and a benefit for the executive, thus linking the corporate agenda with their personal agenda and in life coaching, it ensures that personal goals carry the motivation and the power to change our lives and circumstances.

By taking the time to understand clearly not just *what* we have to do, but the *reason and motivation* behind it any coaching client becomes charged with energy and acts with purposeful and powerful intention.

3. CONTROL: With clarity identified, we should now find a greater sense of influence over our environment. We are now in a position to *choose* our actions and activities.

To be effective, goals or objectives need to be broken down into the smallest of actions or the many steps that make even the greatest of goals work. The smaller the action the more likely it will be accomplished and therefore we can define this as *an action is something you can do when you leave the room* e.g. make a call, make a list, set an appointment, finish a report.

All goals and objectives (no matter how large) come down to the successful completion of the smallest of things. My coaching clients are always surprised by how much they accomplish in a relatively short period of time during a coaching program while still working under the usual pressures of the job.

The secret is in taking these little actions, doing things that they directly control and that they can do when they 'leave a room'. This is important, as a genuine action is not something that be broken down into further actions, it is the smallest possible thing.

Each action accomplished then contributes to the dynamic of success that is builds up, inexorably leading to the successful accomplishment of any goal.

4. CONFIDENCE: With a greater sense of control comes a greater sense of self-esteem and a greater belief in our ability to deliver.

Self-esteem increases when we have clear goals and the power to exercise them. Confidence is boosted by the successful achievement of 'quick hits' or small actions. Success breeds success and with growing success comes more energy to do things, more self-belief and more self-confidence.

Every little action that we successfully complete boosts our self-esteem and subconsciously sets up the motivation to do more. Once we start aligning our focus with our motivation then anything becomes possible. With increased confidence subtle changes also occur in our body language or tone of voice that empowers our ability to influence and persuade others to support us.

5. COMMUNICATION: The first four 'Cs' lead unerringly to the fifth which is effective communication.

Good life and business results come down to the quality of the relationship and the communication between two or more people. This quality is further enhanced by the level of confidence and conviction in the message shown by the influencer delivering the message.

Being confident in what we have to offer, in what we believe in, in our proposal, knowing where we are going (and why) and knowing that we ourselves control the steps that bring us there lends powerful conviction and congruence to our communication and influence.

Personal confidence directly impacts on our body language, our tone of voice and our sense of inner certainty, all key factors to being a powerfully convincing communicator. The essence of good communication in business today can be explained by a simple idea, **C.I.E**.

Connect | Influence | Engage

So how do we 'Connect, Influence and Engage' more effectively?

By learning techniques such as active questioning and listening, establishing rapport, reframing, networking, profiling people and defining their communications preferences and then adapting our personal style to suit them (For more on this check out my book 'The Highly Trusted Advisor: How to Convince, Influence and Collaborate to Lead Teams and Win Clients in the Digital Age').

However communication is not just down to how well we communicate but also who we are communicating with.

For example, in business are we using it to successfully delegate and engage team members or are we managing our professional profile well enough by having a successful communication or branding strategy with key internal stakeholders or our clients? In our personal lives, are we being sufficiently open and present with those who matter to us and enrich or lives and relationships?

Lastly, the final 'C' is:

6. COMPETENCE: Put all of the above together and we come up with top-level performance. The capacity to outlast, outperform or outsell all of our competitors in business, or reach our most cherished personal goals and shape a life that is true to our destiny and dreams.

To be able to provide the best of leadership, services or solutions in the most professional manner to our stakeholders, clients and prospects, that is the mark of success. To be able to live a life well lived, well loved, well experienced and well shared, that is the mark of even greater success.

If Context, Clarity, Control, Confidence and Communication are proactively developed and strengthened then there is a corresponding increase in our Competence or our ability to perform and thus more success and reward.

This is one model I have developed to help define or explain coaching and its place within a complete development program. By giving a client a sense of where they are and why and how they actively manage continuous change, we initiate the empowerment and success of our client.

THE ALPHA-BETA MODEL

For many people without a coach, their performance consists of 'peaks and troughs': highs of performance followed by lows of inactivity, lost focus, lost motivation and poor productivity.

Often we have this kind of performance because we are attempting to be motivated 'away' from something we fear, rather than 'towards' something we desire. This is true both in life and business.

According to the psychoanalyst Sigmund Freud, humans are motivated away from pain and towards pleasure, and there is much value in this concept. In my work I maintain that everyone has a personal agenda that defines their performance and that often, as coaches, we have to help people identify what that is, help them define it and then give them permission to pursue it.

In a basic sense we all have values. These are abstract and global concepts such as freedom, happiness, love and so forth that we are pursuing. These values are powerful in that they define our motivation. However, whether we are living and working in accordance or in conflict with our values determines how successfully motivated we can be.

For most of us, we are moving away from what is contrary to our values (e.g. poverty, dependency, unemployment) so we are driven and motivated by the desire to avoid such things. When such things present a real danger to us we work hard to create an environment where we are free of them. As long as this motivates us we perform successfully. But as soon as we find ourselves no longer threatened by them, we slow down our pace, start to take it easy, lose our focus as the urgency has gone and with it our motivation to succeed.

Then our performance starts to fade and fall off until such time as things we wish to avoid present a threat again. We then speed up our pace, get focused and motivated and performance improves only to fall off again in the course of time. So a cycle of motivation/de-motivation, productivity/no productivity, performance/no performance, boom/bust exists for us. What is lost is consistency, consistency that leads to excellence.

However, if we are working 'towards' values that empower us (e.g. wealth, freedom, happiness), if we constantly reset our sights so that we never settle for what we have settled for in the past, if we learn and are supported to raise our standards and coached to become all that we can be, then performance is different. We become people who create the world that others wake up to in the morning. This is the true power of the understanding of self-actualisation.

When we reach the goals we set ourselves, instead of our performance falling off, we plateau for a short while, enjoy our victories, share the fruits of the journey with our coach and fellow traveller. Then we raise our sights again, towards new horizons, surpassing ourselves in the pursuit of excellence. Becoming all that we can be. This is a journey of continuous self-actualisation.

Let me ask you a question: at the present time are *you* accomplishing everything that you know *you* are capable of accomplishing and reaping the rewards that should go with that? If, like me, the answer is no, then welcome to 99 per cent of the human race. If, by any chance, the answer is yes, then just wait, things will change. Change is life and life is change. We define this simple question with the Alpha-Beta model.

Alpha-Beta Model

ALPHA PERFORMANCE

PERFORMANCE GAP

BETA PERFORMANCE

The Beta level is us, working as hard as we can, keeping up with the pace of work and lifestyle, applying all our energies. The Alpha level is all we know we can be but seldom reach, our full potential. The gap between the two is the *Performance Gap*, what separates us from our complete self, something that we seldom become on our own.

A coach works in that performance gap, helping their client find ways to improve their performance by 10, 20 or even 30 per cent over the existing Beta level. We do this by identifying the empowering values, tying them to specific objectives, breaking them down into actionable chunks and ensuring that the client has the power, the support and the accountability built in to the process to ensure they have the consistency of high performance. I call this 'going from the Global to the Specific'.

The interesting thing is that no matter how far we raise the Beta levels of clients, the Alpha (or fully actualised or 'Flow') level is always impossible to reach: because as the client starts to fulfil and realises the abilities they actually possess, their belief in what they are now capable of (the Alpha level) continues to increase.

So we embark on the journey of helping our clients evolve to ever higher levels through the evolution of themselves. This is about constantly raising the base line. This is about personal and professional actualisation. This is powerful work.

6

A CODE OF PROFESSIONAL ETHICS

For those deciding to go into the coaching industry it is useful to have a set of guidelines by which we as professional coaches conduct ourselves.

In this chapter I outline a professional code of ethics, which all my coaching students are required to subscribe to. In our community, agreement to comply with this code of ethics is an essential part of contracts of engagement.

First, I will outline the individual ethic and in some cases I will add some comments for further clarity.

1. Coaches shall conduct coaching sessions at all times in a professional manner and in accordance with the code of conduct as outlined below.

By 'professional manner' I mean having respect for the client by arriving on time for meetings, dressed in a contextually appropriate (certain industries or environments may have more casual dress codes which it's recommended to identify in advance and match), following up quickly where appropriate and in a state of mind that is conducive to serving the best interests of the client.

---

2. All matters between the coach and the client shall be treated as confidential. No third party shall have access to information given to the coach by the client. Exceptions to the above are (a) when the client has given permission in writing to divulge such information and (b) by force of law.

I always bring this specific section to the attention of prospective clients in the initial complimentary coaching session that I offer. It can go a long way towards convincing them that they are dealing with someone who will protect their interest and watch over them ethically. It lets them know that they are in a safe space.

This can then help to build greater rapport and starts the process of 'contracting' with a potential client. It helps to mention that nothing that occurs during the session will be repeated outside of the coaching room, or shared with anyone else and that, as coaches, we are not here to make judgements. Therefore, they should feel free to discuss whatever they feel has any relevance to the coaching process and meeting their objectives.

Because the coach is trained to be entirely objective, unlike a client's business colleagues, friends or family members, we strive not to be judgmental. As a result, the client should feel relaxed enough to express whatever is relevant to the process. This gives the client permission to open up with information or feelings relevant to making change that may never have been brought to our attention without the security of the promise of confidentiality. The fact that they also have a say in who accesses the information, which requires their written permission, is reassuring and confirms their equal partnership in the process.

The section that covers the 'force of law' is a requirement in the event of a client engaging in illegal activities or issues such as bullying and harassment, safety violations etc. While we hope that this is unlikely ever to be invoked, nevertheless it can be used to protect our professional interests.

---

3. The coach shall observe all laws, have a responsible manner in retaining the good name of coaches by attention to personal conduct, uphold the dignity and honour of the profession and accept its self-imposed disciplines.

This section is self-explanatory but the relevance to self-imposed disciplines is worthy of mention. Because there are often varying standards for coaching and because there is no one agreed standard for the training and certification of such coaches, anyone can establish themselves in this industry and create a business in this field, regardless of competency or experience.

The guidelines that address what to look for when buying-in coaching services if you are in an organisation (see Chapter 8), will serve in some way to filter what has become a rash of coaching services. Unfortunately, disreputable individuals can engage in this business and therefore it becomes important that reputable coaches agree to adhere to some form of self-imposed disciplines for good conduct.

4. Coaches should avoid dual relationships with clients and should never offer their services under terms or conditions that might impair the free and complete exercise of their professional judgement and skill and reduce the quality of their service or risk exploitation.

In short, the coach/client relationship is paramount. Therefore, ideally, a coach should have no personal relationship with a client other than that of a business or professional nature.

While coaching is not therapy and therefore the same traumatic or deeply resonant emotions that are unleashed in the therapeutic environment should not therefore be present, there is always the strong possibility of transference and counter-transference between coach and client. Transference is the phenomenon where there are strong emotional bonds or levels of attraction created from the client to the coach. Counter-transference is where the same emotional attraction is reciprocated or created from coach to client.

While coaching functions with a level of a relationship between coach and client that is entirely dependent on excellent rapport, trust and the willingness to listen and to co-create new futures, clearly there is a level of involvement that may not be appropriate and would hinder a coach doing their job for the client effectively. In short, if there is a desire to have a personal relationship outside the coaching room it is often better to pass the client to another coach, so that the client's best interests continue to be served.

5. The coach shall keep up to date with material and innovation in their specific field and in fields of a related nature to ensure that best practise is applied at all times.

Coaches need to continually keep abreast of developments in the coaching field and in the fields of personal development, leadership, management, sales and business or any areas that relate to their chosen area of speciality. This allows them to bring the best of information to the coaching process at all times. In short, professional coaches should commit to the principle of life-long learning, using every opportunity to expand their knowledge and the resources that they can bring to their clients.

We should commit to the principle of self-actualisation as it pertains to us. New knowledge and new experiences are the stock-in-trade of a professional life or executive coach. They allow us to continually evolve so that the services we then provide are always at the highest possible level and guarantee the principle of 100 per cent.

6. Prior to entering into a professional relationship the coach must ensure that the nature of coaching, the purpose of coaching, the anticipated length of coaching and the cost of the coaching service has been disclosed to the client. No service is to be entered into until an informed consent has been secured from the client.

Caveat Emptor or "buyer beware" has no place in coaching as the client should understand fully the commitment of both coach and client to the process. I offer a one-hour complimentary coaching discovery session, within which I explain the models involved, give the client a direct experience of the G2S process and then outline the financial and time commitments that the client is taking on board. The client must be the judge of the value of the service as an informed judgement makes the process more effective and the results more immediate.

---

7. Coaches will not engage in the provision of advice of a marital or financial nature or in any field in which they are not professionally qualified. They and their clients must acknowledge that coaching is a process of setting objectives, identifying obstacles, mutually agreeing and co-designing solutions and implementing actions that are consistent with improving the professional or personal performance of the client.

Strictly speaking, coaches do not give advice, we ask questions and make suggestions.

Any advice we do give should be relevant to the field of knowledge that we possess and even then, it should be couched as a question, so that the client may give due consideration to the suggestion.

While we need to consider that life balance, the ecology of planning and the personal aspect play a part in professional objectives and performance we should not be there to act specifically as therapists and counsellors (unless we are suitably trained). There is a level at which it is not appropriate to engage with the personal concerns of the client especially if we have not been professionally trained to do so.

8. If during the course of coaching, information is disclosed that would suggest a referral or consultation with another professional would be appropriate, the coaching shall be terminated or deferred and the client encouraged to make suitable alternative professional arrangements.

It is not something coaches are likely to encounter very often if at all, but if, during coaching, a client should indicate through their demeanour or language that there are deeper issues at work and that therapy might be required, the simple rule is this: *if in doubt, refer it out.*

Suggest to the client that there may be issues that they need to resolve before continuing with the process and that this would only help the process further. Be willing to suspend the coaching process and promise the client that they can return to the process when they have had a consultation with the professional they are referred to.

9. A coach shall maintain a duty of care towards clients and shall terminate their relationship with a client when the client can no longer benefit from continued service and shall not provide service if they do not in good faith believe that the client will benefit from the service provided.

Coaching exists to enhance the performance of clients. In doing so, it should attempt to improve the self-reliance and self-dependency of the client. It should not be about creating dependent clients who feel that without the coach they can accomplish nothing.

Usually, the most intensive contact between the coach and the client exists at the start of the relationship. After this, it should be sufficient to offer less intensive continuation programmes that will help us to maintain the foundations of good proactivity and performance.

While dependent clients might sound like a great business idea, it would in due course serve the coach (and the client) nothing. As coaches we avoid burnout partly by being stimulated by the challenge of new faces and new worlds to help create. This is enshrined in section 10.

---

10. The coach should keep in mind at all times that the underlying purpose of coaching is to create improved client performance through creating self-reliance rather than dependency and should maintain the best interests of the client and the profession at all times.

7

THE TOOLS OF COACHING

S o what are some of the critical tools that we use when coaching? What is it that allows us to effect significant change in people over a short period of time? There are two areas I would like to review.

The first set of tools is what one might call the *'Intangibles'* and the second set is the *'Tangibles'*.

The 'intangible' tools are used to shape and create a permission-based coaching environment and the 'tangible tools' are then used to help to focus the often global (or big picture) concerns of a client into specific, actionable steps and define the actual process of coaching.

THE 'INTANGIBLES'

Rapport

Rapport is that indefinable quality that makes or breaks a business or personal relationship. It is often something that is considered an unconscious and hence indefinable process but its importance in any form of relationship is immense. Whether it is a doctor's bedside manner, a friend's obvious respect and concern for us, or a colleague's commitment to a shared vision, rapport plays a huge part in healing, commitment and accomplishment.

No less so than in coaching, where the coach must create an environment in which the client feels sufficiently safe and able to share issues and personal perspectives which the coach must interact with to effect a change in performance.

As part of my work I have effected a significant study into rapport because of its importance in the field of human interaction and it is an area of high priority for coaches in training, for sales teams and for leaders. I spend time helping our coaches in training become proficient at creating rapport in any environment. While it is obviously a quality we all have to a greater or lesser extent, just hoping to create rapport unconsciously is not sufficient in a professional influence-based relationship such as coaching.

It is the responsibility of the coaching professional to create rapport consciously and by choice, with anyone they encounter. I define rapport as:

---

*'that **state** in human relations where there is an agreed, sometimes silent, **recognition** and **acceptance** of **common issues**.'*

It is a 'state' or feeling shared by two people of mutual understanding and respect. Within the coaching relationship, rapport comes from what should be the coach's obvious desire for and expectation of higher things for their client and a common purpose of accomplishing shared goals, the client's goals, the accomplishment of which the coach plays a critical role in effecting.

Things such as body language and posture, breath, the use of the client's words and language, the opportunities for physical touch such as handshakes all play a part in creating a safe, secure and confident environment for the client who is about to undergo a process of change.

Change is a formidable task, it is something that the mind does not readily embrace and so the first step in encouraging such change is to create a protected environment for the client and then proceed with small steps in a sequential process. Rapport is the key tool that allows the creation of such a change-oriented environment.

'Soft' or Influential Language

Matching a client's language and vocabulary is important in coaching because it is how clients express what is meaningful to them. Words, at best, are sometimes inadequate at expressing the full range of our expectations. The meaning they convey is important however and so I train coaches to use the client's positive language to establish rapport and encouragement and to reframe (or change) a client's negative language.

For example, I seldom allow my clients to use the word "try" because when this word is used it becomes a code for failure. "I'll try" might as well be "it won't be done" because inherent in the word is the fact that insufficient effort to effect change will be applied but at least "I tried". So the client must create a clear statement of intent around their work before they leave a session.

It is perfectly acceptable for a coach to use the word "try" however when encouraging the client to try something completely different from their past experiences. This is because even an attempt that fails will help the process of altering the client's perspective on the benefits of a new approach.

Also I encourage coaches to manage the client's use of words such as "I must", 'I have to', "I need to" etc. as these (known as Modal Operators of Necessity) often induce stress-based or short-term motivation.

But 'soft' or influential language is something more again. In the past, language was directive: "do this, do that, this must be done, effect it immediately, get it done, you must/have to do this". This resulted in fear or threat-based motivation, which at best, was only short term.

Short-term motivation needs constant reinstalling in people. In time it creates resistance and even resentment (a clear benefit of using coaching within the organisation is that it creates collaborative management relationships where employees are willing to invest more of themselves in their work).

The language used when creating this therefore needs to be softer, more expansive and inclusive, and is generally couched in questions: "Have you *considered*…? "*If* we were to…?" Where *might* we find…?" "*How would* this be best viewed…?" "If we *were* to look at things differently…?" "*Assuming* that this was possible what would you do first…?" It often involves changing tenses, possibilities and assumptions, identifying and attaching meaning, and the use of what we call the "**inclusive WE**".

The "inclusive WE" is more properly referred to as "Forced Teaming" where the coach immediately begins to speak using the referential index "We", implying that both coach and client are now working on the client's goals as a team.

The coach would only return to using "you" when the client is being tied down to a specific action and we want to clearly hand the action back to the client to decide on or to do.

Using "We" rapidly installs in the client the idea that they are not alone in reaching for these new heights; that now they are being paced, assisted, encouraged and involved in a process of accountability that they have willingly chosen to be a part of for their own betterment.

Attitude

The attitude of the coach is another important intangible in the process. The coach should strive to be:

- be non-judgemental
- be optimistic
- have total conviction in the success of the partnership and the ability of the client to effect the desired change
- encourage an environment of trust by being willing to share relevant personal experience
- be committed to the transparency of the process
- be willing to commit whatever personal resources they have to the success of their client
- have a 'full-on' focus on the client.

The client's success should be paramount to the coach. It demands a great deal from us but there is a great deal of satisfaction in seeing a client develop their potential and success through their involvement with us.

THE 'TANGIBLES'

The tangibles are the specific tools we use when coaching. In defining them, I have also outlined the coaching process used by coaches who train by me.

· · ·

Questions

Coaching begins and ends with questions. In coaching questions are used to encourage dialogue, relax the client and create a conversational environment. However, they have more specific purposes too.

To install ideas:

Questioning the client engages them in the process and as a result they are highly attentive. While they are in this attentive state it is useful to be able to make suggestions which may then be taken on board by the client more willingly than if we were to instruct or direct them.

For example, "Imagine a situation where the problem was resolved and we found ourselves to be more successful, that would be worth taking a small risk for, wouldn't it?" or "Although in the past this may have been difficult, if we were to look at things differently for the future, how might we start making changes?"

Within these questions we are also using 'framing' to put a context (such as "in the past") on the question, leaving previous difficulties where they belong and encouraging the client to take different approach now.

To change perspectives and give instructions:

"If we were to see a new way of doing the job (or living life) more effectively, where might we make a start or what would that look like?" With this question we have encouraged the client to look at their job or personal life differently. We have also automatically assumed that they will do this (a function of expectation). If the client questions this or gives us 'push back', then we might express surprise and restate the question, firmly placing them in a proactive mode and encouraging them to reply with answers.

To help reach mutual agreement:

Mutual agreement is the ideal coaching state. It is where the client is willing to 'try' suggestions that in any other context they might consider too personal, too directive or even too difficult to attempt.

Because questions help us to engage the client, they also convey ownership of the process to them.

We become co-conspirators, facilitators and guides. A client should seldom get a direct answer from a coach. We don't give advice; we just make suggestions. We never make statements when a question will ensure greater client understanding, ownership and hence compliance.

In G2S coaching I created a trio of questions, which begin the process of coaching with all clients. I have called them the *Coaching Trinity*.

The first of these identifies the most important issue the client is currently facing:

At the present time, what is the single greatest challenge that you're facing in the job (or personal life)? or, to restate it, What one thing could we do such that if you were to do it, it would affect the greatest amount of change in your role or career (or personal life)?

Once the client has defined the issue (even at a very high level such as single word or phrase) the answer to this first question then needs to be explored further proactively using other questions to get a highly specific or well 'articulated' goal that we can work with. We are looking to create a concise, clearly worded and specific objective from their answer. The language we use in defining this objective is very important, as it must be positively framed, personal and specific.

The exact language the coach uses when questioning a client might vary depending on the type of client or the level of employee you are working with, but it is essential that we use the client's language and help them shape the words around their goal or objective, as often clients can get stuck in specifying or coming up with the objective's language.

If this is the case, we actively help them with structuring this first and most important objective.

For example if a client said "Time Management" the coach might ask "What specifically do you want to do about time management?" to which the client might then reply "I want to spend more time coaching my team" or "I want to spend more time with my family" giving us a specific outcome or the 'What".

A coach would next seek to *identify the meaning* or the passion the client would attach to reaching this goal by asking something like:

What specifically would this do for you personally, and I don't mean within the job, I mean for you personally? What would be different for you as a result of having this happen?

OR What will you have that you don't have at the moment when you make this happen?

(Students of hypnosis will have seen the embedded command language in those questions) Having identified this, we have now found a structured, written objective with a clear (and most importantly personal) written benefit for its accomplishment

64

attached. It is the one thing that would fundamentally change the client's world as it is at the present. It is the 'Why'.

So the goal would now become (composed now of the What and the Why) "I want to spend more time coaching my team so that I am recognised by my key stakeholders as an effective manager".

We now move to the second question:

What sort of things would you love to be doing in the job (or your life) right now? What sort of ideas or projects would you love to start or create in the role or with the team (or in your life)?

Now we are identifying the things that would really motivate the client and effect real change in their environment (and hence their perception of that environment).

This is where we identify the 'extra' mile that the client is willing to go to change or improve their performance and gain significant personal satisfaction as a result. At this point, we are addressing the things that clients often promise themselves but seldom accomplish on their own. It is here that we start to close the performance gap.

The third question (that to be honest I seldom use now as the first two questions usually are enough to help me identify the two or three objectives that I like to start any of my coaching programs with) is designed to clear the decks, to take everything that should be addressed to the fore and ensure that the client's focus is always on that which will make the greatest change.

What sort of things are you deferring or putting on the long finger that there is no need to defer anymore? Make a complete list of even the smallest things. Let's now get them out of the way.

Out of these questions we have now created a list of things that are critically important and personally valuable to the client at this moment in time. Now we will ask them to review that list, first highlighting with a marker the two or three most important projects on the list and only then sequencing them in order.

Colour and sequence are important factors in creative thinking. Now we have the performance objectives or goals the client will work on and now we also have the client's willing buy-in to the process. Next we have to process the material.

The Competency Wheel (or Wheel of Life)

An alternative to 'the coaching trinity' is the use of a common tool in life coaching called the Wheel of Life. This is a wheel with a number of internal 'spokes' (6, 8 or 10) that dissect the wheel meeting at a central point where they cross over each other.

Outside the wheel and alongside where each 'spoke' touches the circumference of the wheel is usually a horizontal line and on this line is written one of the key elements of a balanced life (health, wealth, family, holidays etc.).

Clients are encouraged to consider each of the 'spokes' of the wheel as representing one of their key values and then to imagine that each line is graduated from 0 to 10, with 0 the very centre of the Wheel and 10 being the point where the 'spoke' touches the circumference.

Then they are encouraged to place a dot or mark on each 'spoke' at approximately where they would measure their present success or skill levels in any of the given areas. 0-3 usually means poor to average, 4-6 means average to good and 7-10 means good to great.

Then they are encouraged to join up the dots from one 'spoke' to the next creating a (usually not very balanced or round) internal wheel. From this the client now has a very good representation of the areas of their lives that need balancing and can then choose a number of areas from which to identify goals to work on.

It can be a great exercise to help a client self-identify where they most want to make change and also provides a visual image of their present situation, one with which they can benchmark their progress against when they do the exercise again either during or after a coaching program.

I often use this in mentoring or team coaching, replacing life values with key competencies of a given role and allowing the person or team to agree a number of competencies that relate to their role or the team's performance. It opens up some excellent team facilitation conversations.

The Objectives Sheet

The Objectives Sheet is stage two of the coaching process. This is what we use to further specify the critical client objectives and the meaning that they attach to their achievement.

Section one of the sheet requests a definition (or a fully formed goal consisting of What and Why) of each of the objectives/meanings that the client is aiming for.

The second section then asks the client to define what obstacles may have held them back "in the past". The use of the phrase "in the past" is important as it indicates to the client that we are attaching no blame to the lack of accomplishment to date. We are also implying that now we can move forward towards accomplishing these objectives in the future. In addition, should we fail to have the obstacles clearly defined and placed on paper where we can control them, we run the risk of having the obstacles remain within the client's thinking as ill-defined anxieties or belief-saboteurs.

Section three of the Objectives Sheet is a listing of the sort of skills or resources that the client wishes to take from the coaching process. In effect, we are asking how they would like to be changed as a result of the process and how they will know that the coaching process has been a success for them.

We have also restored the client to a positive state of anticipation of the outcome of coaching, after they have just taken time to identify what has previously held them back. We always want the client thinking about where they want to be, not where they have been and set clear indicators for them to know that the coaching program has been a success.

The Meta View

The Meta View is an exercise used to change the client's perception, to align it with their new goals and to help them to be convinced that the objectives they have explored are achievable. There are two Meta views: the Meta View 5 and the Meta View 1, the first for five years from then and one for a single year from then respectively.

Because of the longer period of time involved, the Meta View 5 encourages the client to think beyond current boundaries by considering a future five years from now. It is seldom used unless the client is a looking at their personal or life goals or is a business owner and is in a position to shape and create the next five years.

The Meta View 1 is always used as a part of the G2S coaching process and is simply an essay about the next 12 months. We want the client to write about how things will be different as a result of accomplishing their objectives through coaching: what will have changed? How did it change? When was the change first noticed?

There are certain rules to using it. For example it needs to be an essay and not bullet points, the fact that it is based on the successful accomplishment of their goals and how the world will be different and that it must be written in the present tense so that the message is more successfully communicated to the unconscious part of our brain, that is the seat of our motivation.

We also want them to be as specific as possible. The Meta View exercise is based on the understanding that the mind cannot tell the difference between real and imagined memories. As a result of getting the client to write the exercise the coach has now helped install the following into the client's thinking: that the objectives are "do-able" and a clear picture of the benefits to be gained so that their motivation and expectations can start the necessary change to allow them to accomplish the goals.

The mind supposedly deletes, distorts and generalises information. With a "guestimated" data-input of 2,000,000 items per second the mind adopts prioritisation strategies to process only the information most relevant to the brain. Through this exercise, the client is ensuring that the relevant information for their new goals is recognised and fed through to their consciousness so that they can act upon it.

I call this exercise "creative re-programming" or "switching on the synchronicity". A subsequent part of the exercise also allows a coach to access the critical areas of importance to the client which we can then use to motivate them as necessary.

The SMART Goal

Once we identify the critical issues, we break them down even further through the use of

SMART goals. Most people are familiar with the idea of SMART goals - language should be simple and specific, the goal measurable and meaningful, written in the present tense and so forth.

The important points are: that the major goals should be broken down into smaller actions; that a clear picture of the outcome of the goal is generated; and that there is a date by when it should be accomplished. Several goals may be defined, covering diverse areas depending on what is defined as important by the client.

The Action Plan

The Action Plan sheet is used as the tool by which the client is focused on what they need to be doing to effect the change they are looking for on a consistent basis. This sheet itemises the actions necessary to move forward and should include different actions from different SMART goals at the same time so that the client is working on all their goals simultaneously.

The sheet is dated and signed by the client and becomes the means by which the client is held accountable for their actions during later coaching sessions. An important point to note is that I have clients micro-deadline each individual action on the sheet with a completion date prior to the date of our next session. I discovered quite early on that clients who did not have each action dated often returned to sessions having accomplished less than they did when we had them deadline each action. Having them do this brings a greater sense of urgency to the process.

After a number of sessions, one may find that the client has exhausted all the actions they originally defined through their

SMART goals. This is not a problem because if they have accomplished the earlier actions they will have now have created a dynamic that will help carry them to their ultimate goal.

How the action plan is handled is also important. When the client has accomplished an action they are encouraged to place a 'tick mark' beside the completed action which is now a visual and emotive anchor back to school days when they got a correct answer (providing with nice dopamine 'hit' to encourage further actions!).

If an action has not been accomplished then we do not place an 'X' mark beside it, as this may be a visual and emotive anchor back to a negative feeling. Instead we *circle the number of the action* and discuss where the client experienced difficulty. In cases where a client has *not* acted on a specific action, for at least two sessions. then we may need to challenge the client.

In this case, it is useful to ask "just how important" is this to the client (and lose it or keep it accordingly) or to ask them if we need to break it down further to make it more easily accomplished.

Clients often get an early buzz from the fact that they are making real change. Coaches can use this feeling to remind clients of how much more useful it is to be proactive when facing challenges and (of course!) how beneficial it is to be working with a coach who helps them accomplish personal excellence through partnership.

Timing of Sessions

I recommend that professional coaching sessions last about 60 to 75 minutes tops (to ensure we retain their attention) and sessions are arranged initially weekly and then when the client gets to the Action Plan stage, every two weeks thereafter.

When a client starts with a professional G2S coach for the first time, they are usually expected to complete approximately ten initial sessions of usually an hour in duration, every two weeks over 4-5 months or they may have an 8-10 month program (or more) for those in leadership positions. Life or personal or sales coaching can last as little as 6 coaching sessions or as long as a year.

In a company environment the number of sessions will depend on the team member. If they are responding well they may only need to have "formal" sessions once every two/four weeks. If they are not responding well and are obviously in need of greater support, then the coach/manager may decide to work with them on a weekly basis.

In this chapter, I have outlined some of the main tools in a professional coach's armoury and the basis of the G2S system itself. Used correctly, they can effect real and powerful change for clients.

8

INTRODUCING COACHING INTO ORGANISATIONS

Sometimes I am asked about training coaches or mentors in organisations and how best to position either intervention within a firm, so this chapter covers some of the relevant areas when an organisation wants to bring coaching or mentoring into their management style.

While at first glance this may only seem of relevance to those who want to act as executive or business coaches within organisations, it also has important lessons for all types of coaches in terms of client relationships, contra-indications to coaching and ethics so definitely a chapter worth reading.

When introducing coaching (or mentoring) into an organisation there are number of factors that need to be considered:

1. At what level is coaching (or mentoring) to be brought in initially?
2. Where is it best positioned?
3. What are the procedures for vetting suppliers of coaching (or training mentors) services?

4. What challenges will it create for existing managers?
5. What do we do when we face resistance?
6. What happens if there is a conflict of interest between the objectives of the person being coached and the company's objectives for them?

This chapter will act as a guide to answering some of these questions.

Coaching is always best positioned first with the senior management team. The benefits of senior personnel working with a coach are significant, as an improvement in the quality of their performance has significant effects on the rest of the organisation.

Many senior managers often exist in a position of isolation, with enormous pressures for results. They are constantly aware of 'the personal branding and profile issues' inherent at senior company level and the effect that they can have on future promotion. When executives reach the mid-level tier in an organisation they are now involved in what I call 'The Game'. This is where they need to become aware that it is what you appear to do as much as what you actually do that matters for further progression.

Creating an effective and influential network of key stakeholders is important here, people who will support and sponsor your efforts and your brand. For me this is summed up in my 4Ps of the corporate game; **Profile** (build a profile or brand) **Position** (make it known to key stakeholders) **Promotion** (leverage it to get promoted) **Politics** (manage the relationships after you've been promoted).

In all of this an external professional coach or internal mentor, whose sole purpose is to bring an intervention that assists the executive to reach their objectives, can be a valuable resource, a springboard to generate ideas, a person to help them take time to reflect, plan, structure their thinking and launch new projects or even help highly technical executives be more effective on communicating their value and positioning their brand to other key stakeholders.

This situation also gives the executive an immediate understanding of the effect that the coaching process can have on their own managers and teams thereby enlisting them successfully in what can become a cultural shift in the organisation.

However, it is not always possible to access senior management and, therefore, to establish a coaching beachhead one might start with the human resource department. In many cases they will have an understanding of coaching (if not the intricacies of the process) they usually manage the coaching budget and should be able to assist buy-in by critical middle managers. In addition, many firms have coaching panels that a professional coach can ask to be considered for or that go out to tender every few years or so.

Alternatively, sales directors and sales managers can also be excellent initial points of contact as they are charged with delivering on the most critical of business functions. Being such a dynamic

process, sales is an area that readily lends itself to performance improvement through coaching.

The tangible sales returns that good coaching can bring with performance improvement can be especially attractive. In addition, heads of sales may also have a discretionary budget for team development that they can draw from to engage a coach.

CHOOSING A COACHING PROVIDER

Buying in coaching from a potential supplier is an area that also needs to be carefully considered and the coaching provider that an organisation commits to partner with for the provision of coaching for their people needs to be carefully scrutinised. As coaches this is also a good benchmarking exercise to assess our readiness to provide coaching into larger organisations.

To confirm the bona fides of a potential supplier we might ask some of the following sample questions:

1. Do you have a professional Code of Ethics that defines your relationship between the coach and the client?
2. Do you have current professional indemnity insurance?
3. Who are the companies you are currently working with? What industries are they from? At what level are you coaching? What specific areas are you qualified to coach in?
4. What is your training? How are you certified to coach?
5. What models is your coaching based upon?
6. Do you have clients who will speak for you and can we have their names and contact numbers?
7. Are you willing to provide a complimentary initial exploratory coaching session as a means of assessing your skills?
8. What does your coaching programme consist of? What materials are provided?
9. Over what time period is the coaching being provided? Is there a definite start and end date?

If the potential provider is willing to answer the above to an organisation's satisfaction then it's most likely safe to consider them as a seriously supplier. Once the supplier is chosen and agreed upon, we can then begin the process of introducing coaching to the company.

BENEFITS OF COACHING WITHIN ORGANISATIONS

The establishment of a coaching (or mentoring) culture within an organisation can bring a number of potential benefits for that organisation. Listed below are just four key benefits

1. **Coaching Delivers on Training**

Unlike training, which is primarily an educational function, coaching (sometimes in the guise of mentoring) is essentially *an implementation* function. It is about *using* the knowledge gained in the training and *applying it* to effect change. Corporate training budgets are sometimes less effective for the want of the support and supervision that effective coaching would add to the training experience.

Even with excellent training the benefits are often lost when the delegate returns to their original environment where, with no further support, the training manual goes on the top shelf to gather dust and never to be looked at again.

However, when a delegate is coached over a period of time after completing a training the effective use of that learning is significantly increased and the net gain from the training investment to the organisation greatly enhanced. Coaching can in this case, be considered to deliver what training alone can often only promise.

There is a case to be made that training departments in organisations should be tasked not only with the provision of training but with the implementation of that training through regular coaching practice, if they are not already doing so.

Here their specific expertise can be used, together with the normal coaching of the manager, to evolve the employee to higher standards of performance in the area in which they have been trained. Alternatively, the training (or HR) department becomes a centre of coaching resources within the organisation that is able to provide coaching, as required, to support line managers.

For an external coaching professional, there exists the opportunity to offer firms group coaching services, where once an initial content module has been delivered (either live or pre-recorded) then either one or a series of group coaching clinics can be offered to ensure the practical application of the learning in the real world environment. This not only benefits from the coaches professional input but also encourages peer-to-peer learning within the coaching group.

2. **Coaching Builds and Maintains Relationships**

In the past, traditional management did not encourage close relationships between managers and staff.

Management was a directive approach with the manager trained to focus on what the employee did poorly rather than on what they did well. Such a focus often failed to create a collaborative approach to business and instead produced one that played a large part in the "them or us" perspective, a divisive and often self-defeating approach.

Today a more collaborative leadership approach is preferred based on creating partnership between leaders/managers and team members. The emphasis is on co-operation, on shared ownership and on utilising the resources and insights of all members of the team.

The objective is to create a unique synergy between management and staff that will lead teams to new and more inclusive ways of team management and development. The manager now coaches her or his team members to their potential and harnesses that inherent potential to meet team objectives. To encourage team members to explore those hidden resources the manager must be able to build open relationships with her/his team members. There can be no hidden agendas and no power trips.

Effective coaching practice places particular emphasis on the relationship between management and teams. It bases its success on the level of rapport, trust and communication that can be built to create a harmonious and pro-active work environment where, ideally, everyone is acknowledged for their contribution.

This can often be challenging for the traditional manager, as they must now be willing to get closer to staff than ever before so that staff may see their weaknesses and flaws. However, in a coaching environment, such flaws are more acceptable. With the manager acting as a collaborator, facilitator or coach, it is the combined strengths of the team that matter. The most important factors are the positive resources of all contributors that help the team meet its objectives.

Time spent dealing with problems can now be reduced as the coaching relationship allows feedback to be given directly after an event and in an environment of mutual development, rather than mutual suspicion. The effect of this is to reduce time-wasting personnel issues, another significant contribution to company health and welfare.

In a coaching culture, the traditional form of management by punishing mistakes is replaced by a more positive and immediate feedback process, one where both the knowledge of the manager and the event-specific learning of the staff member can be harmonised into more effective work practice.

3. **Coaching Fosters Self-Reliance and Solution Oriented Thinking**

The strength of coaching is that it can offer a systematic process that harnesses the unique strengths of individuals, focused through the coach, to create a solution-orientated and pro-active environment.

In such an environment, people are happy to contribute because they are being recognised and assisted towards their needs through the work that they are doing. Because more meaning is attached to the work, responsibility can be more widely dispersed team. I call this *"autonomy through co-operation",* as with team members now more willing to initiate, the leader or manager is now in a position to delegate further and with greater confidence.

The result is not only increased individual contributions from team members, who now feel that they have a voice in the direction and the results of the team but also the fact that the manager can now work more strategically on the team's goals. The benefits of releasing a skilled manager from having to constantly double-check on their staff is considerable as the manager may now function on their primary task of having the team meet company objectives.

4. **Consistency in Management Style**

In the past, managers learnt many of their skills initially through consciously or unconsciously modelling the behaviour of their own managers. They took on board management habits for good or ill. Add to this management training and their own personality and we have a model of management that can be determined by the conditioning and personality of the individual manager.

This can sometimes lead to an inconsistency in the manager's performance and the operational performance of the individuals that they manage. Many companies have standards that they expect managers to adhere to but the problem can be that with the stress created by more demands in less time, most managers often attempt to get the job done as they see fit.

Coaching can be a simple and systematic process of management. It follows certain easy-to-follow guidelines, has specific co-created outcomes in mind and it creates an environment where all outcomes can be within a realistic time frame. It does not look to the manager to see the work completed but to the individual employee empowering them with a personal reason to see it completed.

It employs both formal and informal meetings as part of its structure. Once the coaching process is employed it creates effective performance and brings consistency in management style.

With such a standard process, an employee transferring between departments or teams can also be managed in exactly the same way as in their previous department. To a great extent, this removes the effect of the manager's personality from the equation, shortening the new team member's learning curve and helping them to contribute more in a shorter period of time.

Areas where coaching might successfully be applied include:

1. Temporary assignments and role changes
2. After training programmes
3. Special projects
4. Developing communication and performance skills
5. Planned delegation
6. Problems and successes
7. Succession planning
8. Time management

CHALLENGES TO INTRODUCING COACHING INTO ORGANISATIONS

Introducing business coaching into an organisation can raise challenges that need to be met in order to effectively implement successful coaching processes. Let's now consider what some of these challenges might be.

Rapid change is a feature of modern business. Business is driven by the next new process or idea and the ability to respond quickly to market forces is the mark of a successful businesses. However, it can be easy to overlook the fact that all change is both driven and managed by people and that the pace of change is different for everyone. Some people are proactive: they create the world in which they look to the next challenge, the next opportunity. Many others are reactive: slow to change: fearful of losing what they already have.

This fear of change can be ingrained in our organisations as well. Some organisations adapt

and respond to challenges with enthusiasm. For those firms who fail to do so effectively, part of the problem is the speed and manner with which information is transmitted through the organisation. They lack the flexibility necessary to adapt quickly.

This can be seen most clearly in the relationship between management and staff. Organisations that are institutionalised and where information is used as a means of control, where highly defined hierarchal reporting structures are adhered to, where seniority is prized over merit, where academic excellence is rated over delivered performance, where old stereotypes are allowed to dominate in the face of the changing nature of the workforce - these organisations face the greatest challenge.

In such organisations, managers have the greatest fear of change and hence the greatest resistance to the idea of a coaching culture, which they see as a threat to their established and rigid management style and their authority over their employees. In today's digital world then these same organisations may lose their best people who opt to leave for organisations that embrace a more open and synergistic management approach that will allow them to fulfil their potential.

The imagined fear of loss as a result of the introduction to coaching, this fear of personal exposure to staff, the greater intimacy and the risks associated with that, are challenges when introducing coaching processes to certain highly traditional organisations (if they still exist of course!).

Fortunately, when I train corporate managers in coaching skills they are assisted in facing these concerns through a series of steps that allow them to prepare their teams for this new style of approach. One of those steps is the initial team meeting where coaching is introduced, critical performance indicators are identified and then allocated to members.

This team meeting not only defines the new parameters but also benchmarks the team through their own feedback as to how the team views its current performance. For the manager, regularly exposed to group meetings, it is a painless way of implementing the initial stages of coaching: from this meeting comes the first stage in creating team/coach synergy and mutual agreement. It is also the first step that ensures they can guide the objectives of the individual in line with the company objectives. In all cases, coaching is designed to create a quantifiable and measurable change in business performance.

The follow-on from this meeting is to use the agreed Key Performance Indicator (KPI) benchmarks or the Competency Wheel (you may know it as the Wheel of Life that we referred to in Chapter

7) as a means of identifying performance targets for an individual team member. This then leads to the first of the one-to-one meetings that begins the process of coaching at a level with which the manager may feel more comfortable. From the individual meeting comes proposed actions that the team member co-designs with their coach, that will positively impact on their performance and have a high degree of personal meaning for them.

When this point has been reached coaching has begun. All that is necessary now is to maintain the discipline of the process through agreed formal meetings at set intervals for the purpose of feedback and re-focusing.

All change comes from action and the smaller the action the easier it is to get agreement to begin. Motivating and generating self-esteem in team members is something that evolves from them through the successful accomplishment of defined activities. In commencing coaching, managers are encouraged to start small, for themselves and their team members. They are encouraged to start with the most co-operative/friendly of staff members. Mistakes will be made at the start and the most forgiving of people are the ones to start with. This allows a manager to build up their confidence in the process.

Managers are often surprised at the initial euphoric buzz that team members get when coaching begins. This is often because, for the first time, employees are actively contributing and feel that they have some ownership of the process. This does subside but what managers then find

is that many employees start to drive the process itself, raising their own personal standards and suggesting new initiatives and ideas. It is then only necessary for the manager to maintain the discipline, the clear focus and re-focusing and the positive feedback to the staff members.

Another challenge to introducing coaching is the need for the manager to maintain the coaching discipline until it is second nature and until it is the preferred management style rather than merely a competency thereof.

Coaching requires discipline. To be successful, it is necessary that the discipline be applied consistently. In the early stages, its success hinges on the disciplined application of the coaching process. This is not always easy. One of our greatest challenges is convincing managers that if, despite the time pressures they are already working under, they take some additional time at the start to ensure that the process becomes a regular and expected one they will save hours and years of stress.

Part of the means by which I encourage the development of an organisation's culture from directive to consultative and by which I support trained managers is to encourage the formation of coaching forums. These forums consist of a group of managers, selected from those who have completed training, brought together to chart the development of coaching in the organisation.

They meet regularly for the purpose of:

1. Discussing the effect of coaching (or mentoring) within the organisation
2. Discussing new ideas or initiatives that have evolved from the workforce as a result of coaching
3. Supporting individual managers in the discipline of its application, taking further training in relevant skills
4. Developing and discussing an internal code of ethics
5. Briefing senior management on coaching's (or mentoring's) benefits in the workplace

In an ideal world, an external professional coach would be involved at two stages after the management team has been trained. First, to continue to provide a coaching service to the most senior members of the management team who would not be willing to be coached by more junior managers and secondly, to provide ongoing support to the internal coaching forum on further developments in coaching or relevant skills.

Challenges to coaching can arise when an individual is facing redundancy or retirement. How can one encourage such staff to engage in the process? The answer lies in how skilfully the manager/coach can harmonise what is most important to the individual regarding their retirement or redundancy with what is expected of them for their remaining time in the company. As long as people can see a direct personal benefit from their actions, they can be coached.

We are often asked, "Can everybody be coached?" Theoretically, the answer is "Yes". But realistically there will always be a percentage of people that confounds the theory. Therefore, in the event that, for whatever reason, a team member resolutely resists being coached then just walk away, do not coach them.

Coaching (and mentoring) should be seen as a means of fast-tracking people, a positive resource that allows a team member to actively engage in an affirmative and personal way with the management and success of their team. If somebody refuses to co-operate they should no longer have access to that resource. In my experience, it is often the case that, as the rest of the team benefits from a different management approach and a more positive work environment, most reluctant employees eventually come around. Coaching should be positioned as a support and an investment and rarely (if ever) as a remedial intervention.

There is an additional point that all coaches should bear in mind when working with their clients and that is that we need to be careful that it can be our expectation or pre-judgement of a staff member's willingness to be coached that is the problem.

Specifically as an in-house manager (less so for the external coach) we may have 'history' with certain team members when it comes to introducing coaching. It is useful to remember that coaching can be a new start for both manager and team and is limited only by our level of expectation of the team. It has been repeatedly shown that staff will rise to our expectations of them.

A branch manager of a building society who had taken my coaching training was not looking forward to introducing his new-found skills to his team. He had worked with them for seven years and felt that he knew them well. He worried that he would face resistance to this new thinking specifically from a particular person who had been with the organisation for many more years than he. However, he persevered with the coaching process, starting with the team meeting and bringing it down to a one-to-one basis.

To his surprise, he found that the staff were delighted with this new personal approach, that their performance levels soared and that they took greater responsibility for initiatives within the branch. However he had been right to expect resistance from this one individual but, as the individual saw the change in the branch and in their co-workers, as they noticed that people were delivering on promises, in the end they too entered the process. Much to the manager's surprise, once this person had embraced the process they became an invaluable source of knowledge and experience, subsequently responsible for performance-enhancing ideas that were applied throughout the branch network.

For us as coaches, helping others overcome the challenge of their limiting expectations can reap significant rewards. Experienced coaches know that they can be very conversational in their approach and therefore can go a long way towards reaching the buy-in that they require from someone being coached before it becomes obvious that a specific process is at work. However, for various reasons, coaches sometimes face resistance to coaching and a person may not be willing to involve themselves in the process.

At this point a coach may need to fall back on their ability to gain compliance through ascertaining the values of a person and using them to create powerful reasons for that person to engage in the process. People are usually motivated by personal pleasure or benefit, so the coaching process can be presented as a system that brings personal benefit to the individual. This is best accomplished by eliciting the individual's values and applying them to the benefits the process can bring to them.

Values are abstract concepts, such as money, promotion, fulfilment and so on, that motivate us towards an objective or away from an objective. As a simple example take someone who says they want to be rich. "Why is that important to you?" we might ask, to which question the response might be, "So that I can care for my family and have a good time."

This is a 'Toward' response as it helps focus the client and their actions on creating a new situation that is positive. However, we might also ask someone why they wish to be rich and the response might be, "So that I'm not poor." In this instance, the person's motivation is to get away from a negative situation.

This negative (or 'Away From') motivation is usually short term and quickly fades when the person has gained distance from the situation they wish to avoid. As a result, is it useless for consistent performance improvement. Therefore, it is necessary for a coach to have the person identify what are the benefits they can gain from engaging with coaching. Language, and the meaning attached to it, is an important issue for both client and practitioner. Using the right words can have a significant effect on a person's performance.

Let's look at the process used when we seek to gain motivation through values.

1. People are usually motivated by personal pleasure and so the coaching process can be presented as a system that brings personal benefit to the individual.
2. This is best accomplished by eliciting the individual's values and applying them to the benefits the process can bring to them.
3. As we may know, values are abstract concepts, which have a motivational direction and are sequenced in a particular order, from which our beliefs about our potentials and ourselves are grounded.

Values are elicited as follows:

1. In the most conversational way possible, ask the person "In terms of the future of our job/role/life what is most important to you?"
2. Make a list of four or five values by getting the most important and continuing with the questions, "And what else?" or, "If there were anything else what would it be?
3. In the event of a negative answer such as "I don't know ask the person to "just suppose" or, "Imagine you knew, what would you say?". Stick with it until you get answers.
4. Then prioritise the values by repeating them back to the person and identifying their order of importance or the "motivational sequence".
5. Then feedback the values in sequence and look for compliance.

6. Finally, build the proposal for acceptance of the coaching process around the client's personal value system, to gain a greater degree of acceptance and co-operation.

CONTRA-INDICATIONS TO COACHING

It is important to note that there may be contra-indications to coaching or indications as to when not to get involved with coaching. Such issues might be:

1. Addictive or dependency issues
2. Marital issues
3. Financial issues
4. Family or personal issues.
5. Behavioural issues

Coaches are not trained as therapists and it is best to remember that if such issues arise or become apparent while engaging in coaching, then the *"if in doubt, refer it out"* rule applies.

Suggest to the client that they may wish to take time to discuss some issues with a qualified person; that as a coach we are not qualified to assist in these areas; and that we can defer completion of the program until they have discussed the issues with others.

We should remember that coaching is not meant to be counselling or therapy: such professions deal with root issues that have occurred in the past and may be affecting current behaviours. Coaches can come in after such interventions and take the client from where they are now to where to want to be in the future. We do not give advice; we make suggestions and bring a unique partnership to help improve the thinking and application process.

At this point it is also worth mentioning the ethical obligation of a coach to both the 'sponsor', which is usually a company funding the service, and the 'client', who is the person benefiting from the process.

On occasion it happens that, as a result of the coaching process the client realises they have no desire to remain with a company or in work role. This is a sensitive situation. On the one hand we have an obligation to the client to do everything we can to help them evolve successfully; on the other hand, we have a duty to the sponsor to assist them to maximise the client's work potential and accomplish the company's goals. So what should we do? We are bound to confidentiality by our code of ethics, so we cannot just discuss this with the company.

My advice to coaches that find themselves in this situation is based on the following points:

1. The client has often resolved to leave by the time they raise the issue with the coach. Therefore, they have already begun a process of mental disengagement.
2. Their performance may not have been all it could have been in the first place as they may have already harboured an unconscious desire for change anyway.
3. The objectives of the company may be improved by having a new, more committed, person within the role.

Therefore, I believe that it is ethical to assist the client to move positions, on the understanding that the needs of the company are met by the client positively contributing to a planned succession and handover process.

This includes the client advising their employer (or coaching sponsor) of their intention to leave at the earliest possible opportunity and once done, we now have a situation where we can meet the needs of the sponsoring company and the client as ethically as possible. Experience has taught me that this is the best method to date.

That and advising the sponsor that situations do occur and that this is my policy when faced with this situation. I would then work with them to decide what policy is best for them, taking into consideration all the ethical and performance requirements. At this point coaching then moves from a performance focus to an exit strategy and succession-planning focus.

9

THE GREATEST COACHING
CHALLENGES

S o what do I find to be the most common challenges I work with my clients? There are approximately seven challenges that present frequently and in different forms when working with both private and business clients.

1. 'IMPOSTER SYNDROME' OR CONFIDENCE ISSUES

Many of the clients in my practice are already successful executives, managers and business principals. They have accomplished much already in their field and yet may still feel unfulfilled. They feel that there is a part of themselves that has yet to be actualised. They are aware of their full potential but they have reached a point where they can go no further on their own.

Their perspective of themselves is no longer sufficient to help them identify their additional strengths and abilities. They may even start to suffer from 'imposter syndrome' or suffer a lack of confidence where they may even believe that they are not worthy of their latest promotion or may be exposed or 'found out' to be lacking or inadequate for the new role in some way.

They often benefit from a neutral and detached view from someone entirely committed to their development and who has no personal involvement with them i.e. a coach. A coach can suggest to them and help them identify, ways to move from where they see themselves as 'stuck'. Often they have reached a point where they almost need 'permission' to access their other resources or strike out into areas they have previously left untravelled: for example, areas of new challenge or new creativity, or areas that might further their personal, professional or company's evolution but that may be radically different from what they have become known for.

This also applies to using their coach as a confidential sounding board for new ideas within their business organisations, career or their personal lives. The coach often becomes a facilitator of their 'future thinking' and helps them by providing feedback and structure on ideas that they may be considering for the future.

2. TIME MANAGEMENT

Time is a precious commodity for everyone. In my practice clients often complain of a lack of time or of the inability to manage what time they have to get the work they need to get done. However, as my friend and mentor Dr Denis Waitley once put it, "We cannot manage time, we cannot make an hour longer than it is or take yesterday back into to-day, so time management is not about managing time, it is about successfully managing our focus."

Coaching is about managing our focus (and particularly our actions and activities) ensuring that at any one time we are using our time as effectively as possible. Coaching encourages us to plan and use each precious moment to carry us forward towards our most fulfilling objectives and also ensures that we stay focused on the enjoyment of the journey.

A useful technique that I use with my clients is to remind them that their most important customer is *themselves*. It is they who contract their time and provide their resources to the company or other people so that the company or their relationships can function effectively. If they were to withdraw their resources the company or the relationship would suffer.

However, despite this we often constantly take resources away from ourselves and provide them to others to our own disadvantage. There are a finite amount of resources that we can dedicate to others until such time as there is a need for payback for ourselves. Unfortunately, we are often too late in recognising this and the payback comes in the form of poor health and/or personal/family problems.

I usually suggest that (in my case) senior executives first take back control over their diary from their personal assistants or predefine strict guidelines on the allocation of time. *We* should be deciding who we see and how often.

We then set up what I call 'virtual meetings', meetings where we block time in our diaries to meet with our most important 'customer' (i.e. ourselves). If we had a request to meet from our most important client right now, we would immediately make ourselves readily available to them, we would not permit any interruptions and we would give them our full attention – so in a 'virtual meeting' where we are holding a meeting with *ourselves*, why would we do any different?

We then use this time to clear the decks of issues, reflect upon current challenges, finish projects, get our reading done and so forth. In the case of a business this is not about time out of or even away from company time; this is an investment in ourselves that contributes directly to the company, allowing us greater professional effectiveness, mastery of work time and the opportunity to develop effective boundaries for our personal time.

3. LIFE / WORK BALANCE

Along with time management, there has been a growing recognition of the importance of balance in our work and professional careers. I often ask career-motivated clients, "Why?" "Why do you do this?" "Why is this important to you?" "What will this do for you?" to be greeted by the answer, "For my family, or kids or my future".

In the current era 'presenteeism' is most likely to be found in the employees of global organisations and industries where uncertainty prevails and where those organisations are operating in multiple different time zones, creating online meetings out of normal working hours.

Burn out of top executives and staff members is no longer an option, nor is it wise. The decisions they make while under unnecessary pressure may impact negatively on the company. The decision they make to leave such a culture and join a more individual-friendly environment could rob an organisation of its greatest competitive edge, the knowledge of its people. High management and staff turnover because of a poor management environment is not something that ensures business success. The company that still uses the phrase "firings will continue until morale improves" is already a dinosaur.

Working with an executive coach is an investment that guarantees the retention of such top executives and management. Keeping them focused on their personal as well as their professional goals is a key tenet of modern coaching. It is the means by which we create high levels of personal commitment and personal responsibility for a company's future in a staff member, when we can show them that the company shows high levels of commitment and responsibility for *their* personal futures.

For personal clients struggling with life and work balance they may be suffering from the pressure of not just their career but also the demands of a young family or a need to care for elderly or dependant relatives, particularly for many female clients who still shoulder much of these burdens as well as maintaining a career. For them knowing when work stops and personal life begins and helping them ensure that they develop the discipline to be able to separate the two (and lose the guilt of doing both sometimes) is hugely valuable.

4. ASSERTIVENESS AND BOUNDARIES

Creating and being able to assert one's boundaries with others is important both in a business and personal environment. Setting limits to what people can expect of you is important for your personal well-being and professional effectiveness. Yet because of the demands that life and business place upon us, we often allow our boundaries to become porous and flexible and find ourselves stressed and unable to cope.

Senior executives and managers (because of the levels of excellence demanded from them) often feel that the burden of delivering on team performance falls on them personally. As a result, they may find themselves carrying out work that their employees should do in the misguided belief that if they do it, it will be done right.

They then fall into the trap of having team members that are either happy to let them take on the burden of the extra work or having others who are dissatisfied because they may find themselves insufficiently challenged and so leave the team, placing further pressure on the already burdened leader. In addition, such leaders often find themselves having further work/projects passed on to them by more senior leaders and finding themselves unable to say "no", as they feel it will create a poor impression and negatively impact on how they are perceived in the role.

In such situations, coaching helps in two ways: first, it shows senior executives and managers a new way to empower their staff and to 'let go' enough to find that their staff are often more competent than they might have believed and more willing to accept responsibility and accountability and secondly, it helps us to create work and people thresholds that allow us to "Say No...For Now". In other words, not to turn someone down flat but to have the courage to make them aware of our current responsibilities/demands and the fact that as soon as we have the capacity we will attend to their needs.

For senior management, I find that assertiveness and boundary issues often relate to their peers. By sharing the latest influencing and communications skills in coaching sessions this challenge can be met by positioning and managing the politics that occur at the highest levels and how the client can best profile themselves to either retain what they already have or further advance their existing position.

Such work is highly confidential and often the coach plays a valuable role in helping the client assert themselves at important times and deal with the political issues that often arise at senior levels.

In personal relationships too, we can often be worn down by the demands of family and friends and lose sight of our boundaries in life.

So this simple technique can be very helpful both in business and life to determine and then assert your boundaries. I call it the MND filter.

Must See (or Do) meaning this is a person or thing of high priority to me and I am always available to them or to do this.

Nice to See (or Do) meaning this is a person or thing of less importance but still of value to me so I will see them or do this thing once the Must See/Do things are complete and lastly.

Delegate or Defer meaning not now, maybe never and not for me!

5. CLARITY

Clarity of thought is essential for productivity. It concerns how we focus and the meaning we attach to the objectives we define. Clarity of thought impacts on the quality and effectiveness of our business decisions and life choices. The fast pace of life today seldom allows us time for adequate reflection. Many of us work reactively rather than proactively, driven by the decisions and actions of others. Without reflection, there is little clarity. Information comes at such a pace and quantity that we often need to be reminded to concentrate on what we do best.

Time with a coach is a regular period of enforced reflection, a time out of time, when the services of such a trained facilitator can enable us to make leaps of insight into our challenges and future dreams.

6. COMMUNICATION & INFLUENCING SKILLS

Technology has provided us with platforms and tools to enhance our thinking, our ability to organise and communicate conveniently and cheaply over vast distances.

The Internet has opened up the world and driven us onto an information superhighway on which we endeavour not to become road kill. It has challenged political systems, redefined relationships into cyber communities, banished nationally-based censorship laws and opened up global markets previously closed to us.

But there has been a downside: people hiding behind voicemails, screening their calls and their interaction with others; automated sales systems that remove the human interaction from the sales process, time zone creep, the increasing use of AI and algorithms. For a time, in this technology fever, we had started to forget about the human factor. But now it is reasserting itself and allying itself to the digital shift to enhance its impact.

This shift to a 'high-touch' economy in the digital 'high-tech' age focuses on the human aspects of business and the inherent potential within the person that helps create the successful teams working in this modern world. The rise of better educated, more motivated and mobile people allied to technological change has meant an even greater need for the human factor, as the world had been in danger of isolating itself into communities of one.

New dynamics have evolved in this 21st century: increased digital-learning; the demand for more high-value sales professionals where the value of the sale is high and the human touch essential; remote teleworkers and clients and managing teams in a new 'blended' management environment.

All of the above require excellent communication and interpersonal skills from the executives and managers who need to lead these dispersed and mobile teams.

Modern professionals have a high need for exceptional communication, influencing and coaching and mentoring skills. They lead through facilitation, listening, influential questioning, synergy, collaboration, co-creation, empathy and all the human skills needed to get the best out of their people and foster creativity, innovation and commitment.

Coaches play a large part in improving the skills of executives, leaders and all professionals and in applying them to the real human challenges they face every day in the process of recreating themselves to face the 'high-touch' era that is here now. (For more information on the skills critical for leaders and sales professionals in the world of today check out my book 'The Highly Trusted Advisor: How to Convince, Influence and Collaborate to Lead Teams and Win Clients in the Digital World').

7. WORKING *ON* NOT *IN* THE TEAM

I have already mentioned that one of the biggest challenges modern executives face is working 'In' the team getting all the little things done that need doing. However, they are tasked to work 'On' the team to get all the strategic things done that take the team into the future and deliver on their targets.

This requires discipline and often the help of an external viewpoint to benchmark the executive or manager's success and their boundaries in this regard. Coaching delivers here by keeping managers focused on the big picture and creating an environment where team members willingly take on the responsibility of their positions.

It is also sometimes useful to remind executives and managers that if they make themselves 'indispensable' to the running of the team (in other words they become seen as critical to that team's success) then they themselves will never be promoted beyond that role!

10

COACHING CASE STUDIES

To get a deeper feel for the variety of work that is often undertaken by an executive or business coach I have included some coaching case studies. The names and the companies have been changed (or omitted) to ensure confidentiality. In each case, more than just the issue commented on here was dealt with through the coaching process but I have chosen specific points by way of illustration.

CASE 1: MARK. GENERAL MANAGER HR.
INSURANCE SERVICES

Mark is general manager of HR for a large financial services company. He is highly experienced, well recognised in his profession and in his mid-forties. When he came to coaching he had been tasked with the job of closing down a significant number of retail outlets, handling the personnel and union backlash from this and doing so with a skeleton HR team, that also had to run all the remaining company HR functions. He is usually a highly focused and competent individual but the stress of the task was beginning to wear him down.

In coaching he found an environment where he had enforced reflection periods in an otherwise hectic schedule. He had a non-judgemental facilitator who helped develop some new solutions to the challenges he faced. He also had an opportunity to try out some new ideas before implementation and the discipline to keep focused on the task at hand.

His views after his programme were that not only had he improved on his usual performance by "30 per cent", but also that he probably could not have come through that period without the assistance of his coach.

CASE 2: GINA. MANAGING DIRECTOR. MULTINATIONAL MEDIA COMPANY

Gina is a young MD with an excellent track record. Each career move she has made has been an improvement on the last. Enthusiastic and dedicated to her work, she was experiencing a crisis of confidence in her position after the introduction of a matrix management structure to the organisation had blurred reporting lines. Faced with a degree of internal political gamesmanship and developing power struggles, she was questioning her effectiveness and her position within the firm.

Her personal motivation was being effected by the change and her future expectations regarding the success of the company were being seriously undermined.

Through coaching, we identified that she did indeed wish to remain with the company rather than seek opportunity elsewhere and that, in the current situation, her work was seriously at odds with her values.

Having recognised this, she was able to remotivate herself to the task at hand, cut the number of direct reports on her management team, change job roles and reposition those who were challenging her and thereby causing dissension. Her confidence rose, her natural assertiveness returned, company morale soared and the haemorrhaging of personnel to competitors stopped.

CASE 3: TOM. BOARD DIRECTOR.
CALL CENTRE OPERATION

Tom is a member of the board of an important call centre operation. He is a very direct person with a clear focus on the task at hand. However, his challenge concerned how he was perceived as a communicator among his peers, direct reports and team members. He wanted to develop greater influencing skills and to be more aware of the people issues that arose from time to time and so stop the turnover of senior management personnel from his team.

In coaching, we psychometrically profiled him and identified his critical performance gaps. Then we began a process of education and role-play during the coaching sessions, where he began to identify the communications styles of the key influencers in his field.

From there we developed a 'character role' that he would use to interact with people. The concept of a role for him was useful as, once he was aware of the roles we all play, he was able to develop a role that would trigger his awareness of the need to be more people focused.

In time, he found his influencing skills improved significantly and the need for the 'character role' was dropped as he internalised his effective new communication style.

CASE 4: NIALL. OWNER/MANAGER SME. MANUFACTURING COMPANY

Niall is in his late forties and the owner of a successful manufacturing firm. His 'hands on' approach ensured he worked long hours and that he was called on for every small decision. He wanted to develop the business further but was limited in terms of his time. He needed to implement computerised design systems and retain critical staff within the firm.

When coached, he started to identify the critical blocks in his behaviour that were holding the development of the business back. With coaching support he gradually loosened his hold on the reins. He promoted people and empowered them through creating 'small step' development programmes. He prioritised his business and client base, identifying the most successful and then axing those that were not contributing sufficiently.

With the freeing up of resources, he was better able to service important clients. Through promotion and 'co-operative autonomy' he increased his retention of quality staff and initiated suggestions from the floor, thus improving the work environment and the quality of production output. He also installed and developed his computerised design system.

All of this was accomplished while still managing the operational requirements of the business. What was added was the difference that better focus and the discipline of being held accountable to himself made for delivering on his plans.

CASE 5: FRANK. REGIONAL MANAGER, BANKING

Frank is a career banker. He loves the work he does and is very conscientious about the importance of his work to the firm. He managed a regional team and was responsible for delivering on their performance. However, in order to do this, he worked fifteen hours a day, five days a week. He suffered from greatly from 'presenteeism'. For him it was important to be seen as 'first in and last out' every day.

Initially he saw no problem with this until asked, "Why do you do what you do?". His immediate answer was "For my family." When questioned further, however, the paradox between spending more time in the office "for the family" and actually not having enough time with his family (a very common work/life balance challenge) became quite obvious.

His long hours were habitual; he felt that unless he put in the hours he wasn't performing effectively. So we began an experiment. For three weeks he would do two 'only' eight-hour days each week finishing 'early', the rest of the week he could work his usual hours. On analysing performance the end of the period he discovered that on the eight-hour days he was by far more productive than the fifteen-hour days. The shortened deadlines put fresh impetus into his work and, therefore, increased his performance.

Over time, he extended the eight-hour period to a daily deadline. He became more proactive about projects, improved his delegation skills, took further trainings and began spending the extra time with his family. He has since been promoted to a very senior role. Where he was previously viewed as being indispensable to the team's success he is now seen as an effective people and project manager.

CASE 6: PAUL. SALES MANAGER. TELECOMMUNICATIONS

Paul, early thirties, was a very successful sales manager in the telecommunications sector. Respected by his team and his peers, he felt that he was not maximising his potential. Ultimately, he decided to leave the organisation he was with because he wished to pursue self-employment.

I then had him advise his employer, choose a suitable successor from within his team and create a handover process that would guarantee a seamless transfer, thus limiting the potential loss to the company. Then I assisted him to exit the organisation and worked with him on developing a new venture, supporting him from the early challenges to where he had created a successful venture within the course of twelve months.

CASE 7: LAURA. SALES MANAGER. FINANCIAL SERVICES

Laura had been a sales manager with the company for some time and was concerned about the fact that she might be passed over for promotion.

While being coached she developed new ideas for her sales team that ensured that they met (and exceeded) target two quarters in a row. She developed new ideas for sales promotion with the client base, including 'hot topic' short seminars, which maximised her and her team's exposure to the client base.

Laura also was encouraged to start contributing articles to industry publications and created her own team newsletter, which profiled her as the 'editor' to her client base and to senior management internally.

At present, she is being considered as a possible head of sales for a new division of the company.

These are just some of the situations where coaching has made an impact. Coaching is about effecting measurable change. In all these cases the intervention and assistance of the G2S structured coaching program allowed people to give themselves permission to release latent potential within them.

Ultimately, it is the client who creates the change, but it is the coach who creates the possibility, the process and the accountability by which it is accomplished.

11

EIGHT STEPS TO C.A.S.H: COACHING AS A SIDE HUSTLE

STEP 1: OBTAIN SUITABLE PROFESSIONAL TRAINING

When I started coaching in 1997 there were no official training organisations available for training and certifying as a coach. However working under the guidance of Dr Denis Waitley, the American speaker, author and behavioural psychologist I developed the unique G2S (Global to Specific) coaching system that I still use today to excellent effect.

Unlike those early days, there are now a bewildering array and varying standards of training providers of coaching some of whom are allied to one of the three big coaching associations; The International Coaching Federation, The Association for Coaching (of which I was Founder Member) and the European Mentoring and Coaching Council who have put some structure and certification to training as a professional coach.

Here are a few pointers if you are seriously considering coaching as a side hustle or a full time career and who might be looking for a suitable training provider.

Any intending coach should have:

- a keen and personal interest in the development of human potential. They should have a personal commitment to helping people improve and reach levels of achievement that they would not accomplish alone.
- experience in the field in which they are intending to coach people. This should be a proven track record in sales, management, general business, leadership, training, nutrition, counselling, finance etc.
- excellent communication and influencing skills and the ability to empathise quickly and effectively with clients.
- clear personal and professional goals for the future and should view the accomplishment of their goals through helping their clients accomplish theirs.
- business development or advanced sales skills if they want to be successful in their own coaching business.

As for a training provider, ideally they should show a proven track record of coaching in the area of the market in which they wish to work (this includes the program trainers). They should:

- demonstrate that the principles of coaching are at work within their own organisation
- be committed to professional standards and have a mission statement or code of ethics that outlines their philosophy to their clients (of which you will be one)
- demonstrate proven competency in the field and should include regular individual or group coaching sessions as an essential part of their training programme. These coaching sessions should at least be over several months in duration - two meetings after a training does not constitute a coaching programme

- be able to show a successful training history and have past clients who are willing to speak on their behalf
- teach a systemised process of coaching that is easily replicable and is effective
- have suitable professional indemnity insurance

If these criteria are met then it is very likely that you can benefit from this provider.

STEP 2: GET A PERSONAL COACH

Should you decide to strike out on your own, then at the very least invest in a personal coach whose style you are comfortable with and who you can model successfully. Find one that can serve as a role model and make it clear that you wish to be assisted to be a coach yourself.

This coach should exhibit the skills that you wish to emulate:

- excellent questioning and listening skills and innovative thinking.
- self-discipline and an ability to build rapport quickly and easily.
- a systematic coaching process (not just a conversational or therapy-based approach)
- an ability to help you identify and articulate relevant objectives.
- an ability to gently but firmly help you to hold yourself personally accountable for your actions and success.

Also consider using a coach who has the ability to remain detached by keeping you to a coaching process over a period of time that helps you accomplish your goal without creating a dependency in you for their assistance.

STEP 3: EMBARK ON CONTINUOUS LEARNING

When you commence coaching you should ideally commit to embarking on a program of continuous learning.

Your ability to be the best of coaches may be determined by the knowledge and the skills that you can bring to each new client. Therefore, it is essential that you embark upon a process of learning on as wide a range of subjects as possible. Professional business skills such as sales, management, communication, technology, career development and all the life and personal skills that are pertinent to your coaching area should be supported by a thorough background of personal development skills.

As coaches are required to help navigate their clients through an era of constant change, they require a knowledge of how and where to access the relevant information at the time it will do the client most good. Read constantly, take seminars and courses, create coaching forums with other coaches and discuss case studies. The first step to being a powerful coach is to gain knowledge. The second step is to apply it for the good of your client.

STEP 4: DEFINE YOUR NICHE

However hard you choose to work (whether having a practice as a successful 'side-hustle' or full time) there will always be a finite number of clients that you can manage at any one time. You will also have a turnover of clients who feel that at a certain time they can no longer benefit from having you as a coach. This is natural and a professional coach would never attempt to create dependency in a client.

To maximise your potential and your earnings you should, therefore, find your market niche. This will be very much dependent on your experience, learning, skillset and personal interest. The per-hour value of these clients and the financial goals you have as a coach may also play a part when defining your niche.

Is your niche sales for example or working with executives, management or entrepreneurs and, if so, in what industry? It is not unusual for coaches to specialise in a particular industry and a particular field of expertise and charge for their value accordingly. It makes it easier to present a business case to a company, as you can show a proven track record in this field and how, through your coaching, a percentage increase in sales revenues or business productivity can more than adequately compensate them for your professional fee.

Is your interest or expertise in developing and empowering people in life, nutrition, relationships, energy or spiritual coaching then the coaching fee might be less but the satisfaction and personal fulfilment can be extraordinary.

STEP 5: ESTABLISH EFFECTIVE QUESTIONING HABITS

Habits are repetitive responses or reflexes. A coach's reflex is to ask questions, in an encouraging manner, with the full expectation of a positive response.

Did you know that there are (at least) six classes of question that can be used in coaching to address different scenarios? Make a study of questions and practise listening. In this busy world people often just need the time and space to talk and the guidance to give themselves permission to make extraordinary changes for themselves and their companies.

STEP 6: BE CONFIDENT TO BE INQUISITIVE AND DARE TO CHALLENGE

Coaches walk the talk. Our job is to take people from their comfort zones and put them in a place of personal and professional fulfilment. In the pursuit of this goal, there should be no 'No Go' zones (the exceptions being medical, financial or marital advice or areas in which we may not be qualified to give counsel and that are defined under your code of ethics).

We should have an abiding expectation of and conviction in our client to make just the change they need and we should be as probing as is necessary to help them see that future too. They may push back on us, even clients who engage with us willingly may fight us when it comes to accepting change. So be prepared to challenge them hold them to their goals. That is our job, to help navigate clients to shores they may never have reached alone.

STEP 7: COMMIT TO PROFESSIONAL ETHICS

In an industry that all these years later is still shaping itself, a personal commitment to acting in accordance with a code of professional ethics, one that espouses a duty of care towards clients, is an essential step. As with many emerging professions, there are few guidelines on how clients may choose a suitable business or personal coach. Anyone can set up a coaching practice just by hanging out a sign. Fortunately, coaching is one of those areas where results matter and where such results can be measured and quantified. This itself should eventually weed out those coaches who fail to give their all to their clients.

To establish credibility, it is useful to indicate to clients that we bind ourselves to a written code of professional ethics (perhaps similar to the one I have outlined earlier) and provide them with a copy of such a code by which they can measure our performance for them.

STEP 8: BEGIN. START NOW

Coaching is a proactive process. It demands the highest degree of proactivity from the coach. If coaching is for you, begin now, whether as a 'side hustle' to suit your time or lifestyle or as an innovative and entrepreneurial style of management, throw yourself all the way in and go for it.

Coaches are those who help shape the world that others wake up to every morning. It is a growing and an important profession and industry for this century. In time, it will fulfil what I believe to be its most important purpose, a purpose greater than employee satisfaction, or better productivity, or more effective management, or better work/life balance, or learning organisations, or career or meaning in life and work. It will help people on the way to their most important quest in life: to become everything they are capable of being.

To change the world for good or ill, we first begin with a single will. The first will to begin with is our own.

Enjoy journey.

The END

Sean Weafer
Dublin, Ireland, November 2020

If you would like to explore a route to 'C.A.S.H: Coaching As a Side Hustle' then consider joining my coaching school to certify first as a CPD certified G2S Coach and then in the High Trust Advisor business development/management program, both to support you in building your practice and your clients in the skills needed to lead teams and win clients in today's world.

For more details on certifying and training as a professional coach with me visit www.SeanWeafer.com

ABOUT THE AUTHOR

Sean Weafer is an international executive and sales performance and communications coach and professional conference speaker / online facilitator who specializes in turning executives, experts and professionals into highly trusted advisors who can lead teams and win clients in the digital age.

Sean is an engineer by profession and can take complex concepts in leadership and sales and create highly practical and measurable tool kits for his clients to help them excel in all areas.

He is the creator of the G2S coaching system and a certified coach trainer, he is also a Marshall Goldsmith certified leadership coach and a qualified psychotherapist.

He lives in Dublin, Ireland with his wife Sharon and his two sons Nicholas and Gregory (and Kai the family pet dog). He has a keen interest in history (Roman and Viking-age), movies, personal and spiritual development and is a horseman and martial artist.

You can see some of Sean's speaking presentations, master classes and tips at:

https://www.youtube.com/user/SeanWeafer/videos

Connect with him on LinkedIn at Sean Weafer

or join his High Trust Advisor Network on LinkedIn

Contact Sean at sean@seanweafer.com